THIS LOVE

VOL #1

"Love That Covers A Multitude of Sins"
1 Peter 4:8

Mrs. T. Jackson

"Therefore, what God has joined together, let no one separate." Mark 10:9 (NIV)

This Love "Love That Covers A Multitude of Sins."

Published by: Divine Book Design & Consultants
Website: divinebookdesign.com

TABLE OF CONTENTS

INTRODUCTION

When I began to ponder about the marriages within my family, I started to see patterns of follies, chaos, and destruction—a trail of divorce, abuse, or adultery. One day, I had the pleasure of talking with my grandmother about her past, digging deep into details regarding her mother's marriage (my great-grandmother). I shared with my grandmother a story my mother told me regarding a time when she (my grandmother) had left her husband after a heated, physical argument and called her dad. I was interested in knowing who Mr. Davis was because my great-grandmother's last name, to my knowledge, was different. My grandmother smiled and said, "Well, you know, back in those days, you married young, and the gentleman would come to ask your father or parents for their daughter's hand in marriage at around 12 or 13 years old. Young girls did not have much say in the matter. Therefore, Mr. Davis was my daddy, but they had divorced by the time I was married." She smiled shyly and said, "Yes, I remember I tried leaving, but ole Frog came and got us." (My grandfather's nickname was Frog). She was still smiling as if this was a happy memory. At that moment, I believe she felt proud that he came back for her, loved her, and did not want to be without her.

I went on to inquire about when she first met my grandfather. I never had the privilege of meeting Mr. Frog (nickname) because he had passed away at 35. All my mother knew was that he had gotten sick, went into the hospital, and never made it back home. It was a tragedy for my mom to lose her father at the young age of around 15. To make matters worse, their home caught fire on the day of the funeral, burned to the ground, with no pictures or any memory of my grandfathers to keep. My grandmother told me she met Mr. Frog at her mother's beauty shop, "up yonder," as they called it back then, up there on the corner of Shelby. He would come by to get his hair washed and trimmed. She was working in the shop sweeping and cleaning, and he would always ask about her. She said, "he was checking me out," with a big grin.

My grandmother had ten children with Mr. Frog; she lost one during birth, who was stillborn. She had seven girls and three boys. I heard them all reminisce about how their dad would love to go out and party, while he also was heavy on alcohol. My grandmother would have to stay home with the babies while he was out. Upon returning home, he would want to fuss, cuss, and fight several times. I have been told that many of the men on my grandfather's side were in some way abusive, drinkers, and had been known to tip-toe around with other women who were not their wives. Being mindful that this was the earlier times of the 1900s, the Black men in that day had a lot of oppression to deal with, and sometimes it was handled poorly.

I started seeing a pattern of either divorce or abuse within my family. I also noticed a strong force of independence that seemed to arise among the women in the family. Perhaps due to the things they had come to know and witness with men of their surroundings and somewhere along the line, decided they did not have to put up with it. Among the children, one marriage lasted; however, many would have wondered how and why. I am learning it is by God's grace, love, and design for this kind of love to last.

The devil is against Godly marriages and families. It has been his goal since the fall out of heaven to taint, pervert, and destroy the plan of God on families. God's word says, "It is not good for the man to be alone. I will make a helper suitable for him." Gen. 2:18 (NIV)

The Word continued saying:

Then the Lord God made a woman from the rib He had taken out of the man, and He brought her to the man. The man said, "This is now bone of my bones and flesh of my flesh; she shall be called 'woman, for she was taken out of man." That is why a man leaves his father and mother and is united to his wife, and they become one flesh. Gen. 2:22-24 (NIV.)

Marriage is sacred, a commitment, and a bond that should not be easily broken. Marriage between man and woman being fruitful and multiplying the earth can bring forth generations to worship and praise the Lord. The devil wants to destroy as much of that as he can, for the Bible says, "The thief comes only to steal, kill, and destroy." John 10:10 (NIV). Therefore, the devil is trying to steal husband and wives away from each other with chaos, foolery, and deception, whereby killing the marriage and destroying the family all together if we let him.

My grandmother did remarry some years later to a man I got to know for a small part of my life as a grandfather. In my eyes, he was cool and fun.

He would always give me .50 cents or buy us (the grands) some ice cream from the truck. I do not recall ever seeing him angry. I remember him and my grandmother being loving; they would fuss, but it was a cute, regular husband and wife fuss. I remember saying to myself that they love each other. He died of a heart attack when I was around 10, and my grandmother never remarried. My grandmother told me she met him at work, and he pursued her as she smiled again. She said she initially disliked him, but he was persistent. My grandmother's nickname was Chasey, and my uncle would say he believed they called her that because she would have the men chase her around; in other words, I guess she played hard to get, as they say.

During my childhood, I learned about marriage by watching my grandmother, my parents, and my aunts and uncles' relationships. I asked my mother how she met my dad, and she told me that his cousin was dating her sister, and he was told that all her sisters were pretty. My mom's sister told my dad about my mother, and he wanted to meet her. It was love at first sight for my dad, according to their version of the story. My dad was in love with my mother's beauty. However, my mother said she was uninterested in him; she felt he was too old and too big (heavy.) He was nine years older than her and had already been married and divorced but with no children. My father had to persuade and pursue my mother. My mother's sisters also coached her to marry him, saying he had a good job, a nice car, and would be able to take care of her, and that he did.

My father pampered and took care of my mother. He bought her a house, nice furniture, all the nice clothes she wanted, and a nice car to drive; she did not lack anything. Soon after they got married, my oldest sister was born, and from what I am told, those years were great for a while; then the chaos happened! Sneaking, cheating, and lying had crept into the relationship. My father started wanting his old life back, running the streets, catching the ladies' attention, and playing the field, as they also say.

Remember I mentioned a strong force of independence had begun to rise in the women of the family? Well, my mother said she had seen too much hurt, dirt, and abuse, and she was not going to stand for it, so the fighting began. My mother thought, 'If he could do it, I can do it too.' The situation got messy! My eyes are tearing up as I write, remembering the many horrific fights. Let's be clear: my mother was not a walkover; she went toe to toe like she was in a boxing ring. She would mouth off repeatedly, and I would pray she would be quiet because I did not want the fighting to start. Mind you, I had seen my aunts and uncles fight with their spouses, not just arguing but physical altercations; that is torture to a small child learning what relationships are.

The fights in my house got so bad, and I remember one day, my sister and I were lying in our beds listening to the quarreling coming from our parent's room to the hallway. Suddenly, there was a loud boom, and our door flew open. I was crying and yelling, "Please stop," and the next thing I knew, my dad slapped my mom, and she pushed him so hard (*my dad was over 6 feet tall and over 250lbs*) that he fell into my bed, causing me, to fly back and hit my head into the wall. The incident caused a huge knot on my head, and they still fought. During those terrible years, there were some scrapes, bumps, cuts, and bruises, and then my parents finally divorced.

Marriages were destined to fail within my bloodline, an indication of a generational curse. What is a generational curse, you might ask.

Well, according to biblestudy.org, **Exodus 20:4** states:

"You shall not make for yourself an image in the form of anything in heaven above, on the earth beneath, or in the waters below. You shall not bow down to them or worship them; for I, the Lord your God, am a jealous God, punishing the children for the sin of the parents to the third and fourth generation of those who hate me, but showing love to a thousand generations of those who love me and keep my commandments."

Also, **Exodus 34:7**, *"Yet he does not leave the guilty unpunished; he punishes the children and their children for the sin of the parents to the third and fourth generation."*

This seems to cause one to think that this is not just learned behavior but perhaps a spiritual yoke, oppression, or enslavement that had been passed down through the generations of my family, with divorce, and if not divorce, then a strong force of abuse or early death. You may ask the reasons for such a harsh curse. It is simple: God hates sin.

In Proverbs 6:16, the Bible speaks of six sins the Lord hates and seven that are detestable to Him; this chapter warns against follies. Of course, some would say, "But that is the Old Testament." True, but we learn from the entire Bible, from cover to cover.

Regarding generational curses, there is good news! The curse can be broken for those who believe and accept Jesus as their Lord and Savior because it has already been broken through the blood of Jesus Christ. The Bible states that "Christ redeemed us from the curse of the law by becoming a curse for us, for it is written: "Cursed is everyone who is hung on a pole" (Gal. 3:13). Gaining an understanding of some concepts of law, for example, in the justice system, one may have been arrested and had to be proven not guilty in the court of the law before a judge, and the jury finds the evidence of one deemed not guilty. However, the residue or the arrest remains on one's record. Therefore, one may have to go through legal processes to have their record expunged. This would be my view of generational curses: The wages of sin have already been paid, but the legal residue of that curse may still be lingering dormant, waiting to manifest again. One would need to clear up any legal ground that may have manifested through sin. We do so by pulling down those strongholds present in one's life through repentance and commanding these spirits to leave you by the blood, power, and authority of Jesus Christ.

Jesus rebuked the impure spirit when he saw a crowd running to the scene. *"You deaf and mute spirit," he said, "I command you, come out of him and never enter him again. The spirit shrieked, convulsed him violently, and came out."* Mark 9:25-26.

I had to learn this after I was married and started seeing a pattern within my marriage. When I knew and realized that the devil was trying to destroy my marriage, I had to tell the devil, "You cannot have my marriage, and you no longer have that right to afflict me, for I am FREE!"

Let us begin the journey of seeking love!

CHAPTER 1 | YOUNG RELATIONSHIPS

Let me reflect on my life before I got married. I was young, in high school, and just learning about the dating and relationship scene. I battled low self-esteem and often felt unattractive because I wore thick glasses. My family teased me for having a high yellow complexion and sandy-red hair tone. They frequently called me white, albino, adopted, four-eyes, or blind as a bat. I thank God for my journey because He sent a ram in the bush on my behalf.

My mother was **my cheerleader**, always telling me I was unique and pretty, that people were just jealous of me because of my skin tone, and how people were trying to dye their hair to have my hair color. She often told me that I am blessed and I can succeed. She would call me "Foxy Red." One of my uncles, by marriage, would always call me pretty. He would say, "Come here, pretty girl." He would tell everyone that I would grow up and be a model. I thank God for him and my mother; they gave me strength, built my self-esteem, and I started believing I was beautiful. Eventually, my body developed, and I had that Jennifer Lopez shape, but maybe not as much.

When I finally started dating, I thought I was in it for the long haul. It was me and that person until they began to act funny by not calling much, not visiting much, and having few conversations. In learning from my older sister and family members (*remember the strong-willed women in the family*), I, too, said, "I do not have to put up with this," and it was on to the next one. I did not have much time for heartbreak; I felt like I could get another boyfriend with no problem (*without using sex for a reason because I thought I was cute by now*). My perception was, "Don't ever think that you are irreplaceable.

This mindset continued until I met someone I thought was the love of my life at that time, but I was wrong. I remember him being in my 8th-grade class, but I was not paying him any attention.

I was introduced to him (Arthur) one summer by my best friend, who had started dating his friend. They lived about three blocks over, and we would sneak over there every little chance we could. My best friend's father was very strict. If we asked to go to the store, he would put a time limit on it, and if we asked to ride our bikes, he would also give a time limit. Knowing what I know now, I see why he did the things he did; he was a smart man. If my best friend had returned later than he had stated, she would have been on lockdown for about a week or two. As for my house, by this age, I was allowed to go back and forth with just checking in; no limits except being home by the time it was dark. Because I enjoyed being with my best friend, I was also consumed by her time restraints.

When we got a break, we would run as fast as we could to see her boyfriend. Arthur would talk to me while they were hanging in each other's faces, but I was not initially interested. He was nice-looking but seemed more interested in getting someone to sleep with him, and I never wanted to be considered fast or easy. I had heard people call my sister fast, and it made me upset, so being the middle child, I had learned to make sure a guy would work at wanting to be with me, and if he truly liked me, he would be respectful and not let intercourse be a factor.

I had met guys who had the wrong intentions. One guy I thought liked me until he tried to talk me into going into an abandoned building with him, claiming that there was a mattress inside. My head turned around, and I asked, "Are you crazy? Absolutely not!" He said that if I loved him, I would go with him and do this to prove my love for him (*we were in the 7th grade, mind you*). That ended fast, and I thought I learned not to trust so easily. I watched how my cousins treated some girls and would talk about them after they got what they wanted from them. Listening and learning taught me not to go that route.

Before I met Arthur, I had a little boyfriend in junior high after that creep who tried to get me into the abandoned building. His name was Terry. Terry appeared sweet and pursued me with charm. He carried my books and lunch tray, wrote little love notes, and walked me close to home (*I could not let my dad see no boy walking me home*).

Eventually, I said yes to being his girlfriend. He was fun and would defend me, but he sometimes had a split personality. He would get mad and talk randomly about my glasses or the color of my complexion or hair and would be mean and pushy. He would later apologize to me; it was just strange. My female cousins could not tolerate him. When they stayed at my house, we would ride our bikes over to Terry's house *(always staying outside)*, and he would show out and act stupid in front of them. However, when we were alone, he was a sweetheart. I even got my dad to talk to him so he could walk me home and visit occasionally. He was the first guy to come over to my house.

The so-called relationship lasted until around the middle of my 9th grade. Terry failed a grade and stayed back at junior high school while I went to high school. Terry wanted to break up; he thought it would be best since we were not in the same school anymore, but I insisted it was unnecessary. I told him it could work. I did not want to start my freshman year without a boyfriend. I wanted to say, "I got a man" to anyone that may have asked.

Terry and I remained friends during my adult years; however, he had some issues in the end. He was cool, but we were not meant to be together.

Reflecting on my time with Arthur, I always laughed and flirted with him when I went with my best friend Cece to see her boyfriend. He would try to get me to go to his house across the street, and I would ask why. He would always say, "You already know, girl." I would behave ignorantly and ask if we would play cards, chess, monopoly or if his parents were home. Whenever he said no, I would tell him I could not go to boys' houses whose parents were not home. I remember him asking for my number, and I told him I could not have boys call my house (which was not true because Terry was calling at the time).

One day, Arthur and my best friend's boyfriend came to Cece's house, and she told Arthur where my house was. He had the nerve to knock on my door. I told him he had better be glad my father was not home because he did not play. I think that was when I gave him my phone number, but I told him I had a boyfriend named Terry.

He responded that he was also seeing someone, so it was not a big deal. My face felt like it was smudged in because I was not expecting him to say he had a girlfriend. Our situation made him even more interesting for some reason.

We became very good friends, mainly through phone conversations. He would tell me he liked me and ask to be my man. I would remind him that I got a man, and he would say, "So why are you talking to me, though?" I would also tell him that I did not want to date anyone else who went to the same school as me because I did not want any problems with other females or him trying to spread my business.

I ran into Arthur in our school lounge cafeteria when my freshman year started. A song by a group called Whodini was playing. The song was called "Friends," and I sang it very loudly. He was sitting to the side, and I looked at him, kept on singing, and walked past him. Later, he reminded me about what happened during the day and how he thought I was cute.

We continued being like best friends, talking all through the night, watching T.V. shows together over the phone, tripping out, and acting stupid; I really liked him. He would share stories of his girlfriends, and I shared mine, and we would advise each other.

My relationship ended with Terry after he learned I was dating Tom. I met Tom in the spring of 9th grade, around the same time I started talking to Arthur. I learned about Tom when my cousins and I visited an amusement park. My cousin Shelly had met a guy two years older than her, and he introduced me to Tom. Our conversations were over the phone; I never met him until my little sister's birthday party at a McDonald's near Tom's apartment. This was on the other side of town from where I lived. When he came, he had a group of friends, and I was with my cousins, but after they saw us, they all ran off. That night, he called me and said he was scared I would not like him. I told him I thought it was the other way around, but he said no and asked me to be his girlfriend. We still hadn't seen each other for a while after that.

One day, I went to see Terry and forgot that I had written Tom and S all over the side of my sneakers. When Terry saw it, he was livid. He removed my shoes and threw them in the bushes, which was how our relationship ended.

*****

Tom was two years older. He was smooth and had a nice voice. I felt cool talking to someone more mature, or so I thought. While Arthur and I remained friends, I started dating Tom. My older sister had moved to the other side of town, close enough for Tom to walk over to her apartment. I started hanging out at my sister's apartment, and he would visit while my cousins were there with me. One Saturday, when my sister went out and allowed my company to stay *(big mistake)*, I was pressured into playing a game of house, which led to me losing my virginity. It was not a big emotional thing; I felt like I was pretending to be someone I was not. I wanted to be the "cool chic" who knew what she was doing, based on reading adult books I found, cable television with "R" rated programs, and listening to other people.

I never told Arthur that I had lost my virginity because I did not want him to think less of me or that I was easy.

When winter came, I saw less of Tom; the so-called relationship was dying, and I was not interested anymore until one very cold winter night, he wanted to come and visit me. By now, my sister had moved out of town, and he had to catch a few buses to visit. We did not know the bus line didn't come to my sister's house, so he had to walk the rest of the way in the dreaded blizzard-like weather. When he arrived, he tried to take advantage of the situation, and I wouldn't say I liked it, nor was I comfortable with it, so we broke up shortly after.

When I got older, we remained friends for a while.

CHAPTER 2 | HIGH SCHOOL LOVE

I was in the 10th grade after the relationship ended with Tom. I hinted to Arthur that I was single. He had moved to the other side of town and no longer attended the same high school as me. This was the perfect opportunity to date, so we officially became a couple. I believe he thought I was bossy and confident because I told him I would not remain single for long if he did not take the opportunity at hand. I was confident because several guys were starting to like me.

Reflecting on those years, I clearly see I was acting too grown up for my age. I was in the 10th grade and was 15 years old.
I thought our relationship was the best because we were friends before we started dating. He knew how silly I was, what I was afraid of, my

likes and dislikes, shared secrets and desires, and I trusted him.

Arthur would visit my school from time to time *(I don't know how he never got caught trespassing)*. We spent much time together at different places, including my home, even though we had to sit on the porch *(no boys allowed in the house)*. We would also meet at the mall or downtown.

One Friday night, I told him I always went to choir rehearsal on Saturday mornings, and he asked where my church was located. We discovered it was just a few blocks from where he lived, so we started seeing each other more frequently. He would come over to watch us rehearse or meet me outside after we finished. I loved having him around, and my cousins liked him as well. However, after a while, they were tired of seeing him around; it felt like he was taking my time away from them.

Eventually, our relationship got stronger; he was my world. We dated through 10th grade. We talked, played, and laughed a lot *(we were both very silly)*.

After a while, I started babysitting my God sister's son; he was about two years old. My God sister had moved a few blocks from where Arthur lived, making it easy for us to see each other. One weekend, I asked if he could stay at the house with me while she went out, and my God sister agreed. She had already given me the talk, and she knew that my older sister had found out about the relationship between Tom and me. My sister coaxed me into getting on birth control, and she threatened to tell our mom if I did not comply. I agreed to her request, but she still told my mom anyway. It was cool, and I preferred not to have the secret haunt me anyway. My mom told me to be safe and responsible.

Arthur came over, and he was good with kids being silly and playing with them (*Based on my observation, most children liked him.*) After putting my God nephew to bed, Arthur and I got intimate. From that time, I knew he was the one, and we would be together forever.

We continued dating through my senior year; however, we broke up due to me finding out that I had contracted an STD, which is a common STD that can infect both men and women; it can cause serious permanent damage to a woman's reproductive system. Per the CDC *(Centers for Disease Control and Prevention),* anyone who has unprotected sex can get chlamydia. However, sexually active young people are at a higher risk. This is due to behaviors and biological factors common among young people. I found out I had this STD because my older sister made sure I was getting regular checkups. She was working as a Medical Assistant for an OBGYN doctor. On this occasion, Arthur decided to accompany me to my appointment *(little did he know how the tables would turn).* When the Dr. came in and told me the results, my face was in shock because I knew it had been over a year since I was with someone else and had been checked since then, so the only person who could have given it to me was Arthur! My Dr. called him into the room, and she asked him if he had been sleeping around with other people. He said, "Aha, no," knowing good and well that he had. She eventually got it out of him because she explained how often I came to do my checkups and that I had always been open and honest.

Arthur admitted to cheating but stated that it was an accident and a one-time affair. He blamed it on the alcohol. I was furious, disappointed, and embarrassed, but I was crazy enough to forgive him. This would be the case of crazy, foolish, and blinded love. We broke up but got back together after his begging and pleading. Yeah, he was sorry, alright.

In our senior year, Arthur did not go to school. He stated that he did not like school, that it was boring, and that he did not want to be there. I was determined to graduate and started looking at the possibility of college. I say this because during the early years of my childhood, during the time of my parent's separation and then ultimately their divorce, I was having a hard time in school. We had moved a few times, and I went to several different schools. I could not focus, and my concentration was very low. I was timid, scared to talk to people, and very reserved. I was eventually labeled with a Learning Disability.

I attended smaller English, Science, and Social Studies classes from elementary to high school. I could have tested out of these classes by high school, but I had gotten so used to the smaller classes, and for the most part, it continued to be the same group of students with me, and I did not want to leave. I was also afraid of failure; therefore, I would flunk the test on purpose.

When I got to my senior year, my older sister, God sister, and the career development coach at my school encouraged me. They told me I was smart and could achieve anything I wanted. Because of their encouragement, I start considering having a college degree. My cousin had already gone off to college for her two-year degree, and she was able to give me some insight. No one in our immediate family had earned a college degree, so this was a big dream I wanted to pursue.

The career development program blessed me with a few odd clerical jobs. Still, I finally got a breakthrough in my secretary studies class to work in a student career program for the Federal Government. I was in school for half a day and worked the other half. I was maturing fast, and Arthur was in the same place of going nowhere and doing nothing. His family problems somewhat hindered him, but he could have persevered if he wanted to. There was some friction in our relationship, and we broke up again and saw other people, but we made a pack not to be intimate with anyone else *(I was silly enough to believe it)*. I later discovered that Arthur was dating other girls, so I started talking to other guys.

I met a nice young man named Clinton, whom I liked. He was sweet, charming, and respectful, and he was all about treating a lady like a queen. He was a few months younger and a grade lower than me, but he had dreams and wanted to be somebody of value. When I met Clinton, I wanted to have my driver's license for prom, and my dad had purchased an old 1978 green Pacer for me; it was so ugly. Clinton tried to teach me to drive, but he was unsuccessful. Unfortunately, I was a difficult learner; driving was hard for me. Unfortunately, I had to pay for private lessons twice before getting my license, but not in time for prom.

I eventually ended the relationship with Clinton because one of Arthur's cousins was talking to Clinton's brother. Somehow, someone lied and said that I slept with Clinton, and I was convinced that he was the one who started the rumors. After discovering he did not say those things, we made up and remained friends.

The next guy I met was Tyrone. He was older than I, about two years older, and had already graduated, but he had a son by his high school sweetheart. He eventually joined the Military and even asked me to marry him *(we had never had sexual relations),* and I respectfully declined. He was sweet, kind, and caring; He even tried to teach me to drive, but I was not in love with him. He wanted to take me to prom and offered to wear his Army uniform. However, I declined that offer because I had gotten back with Arthur by then.

I finally encouraged Arthur to get his GED at an institution that also offered a certificate course in welding. By this time, it was graduation, and I needed him to have a plan.

We went to my high school prom together, and I was elated. My sister got us a limo. It was originally supposed to be a Rolls-Royce, but the company called the night before and said they had a mix-up in the scheduling and that I could ride in the Rolls-Royce with other people. I was so upset and told them that would not work. I was not fond of some of the people I went to school with, so I did not want to ride with them. However, my sister's boyfriend managed to get us a regular limo with a limited time span.

We had to leave on time to get to prom 30 minutes early. We were the first students to arrive, so we walked around the hotel for about an hour before returning to the event. I was so excited that my best friend Dee, the only close friend in my class, was coming to the prom. I did not have a lot of friends in High School and would have no one to talk to if she did not show up. Initially, she did not plan to attend because she was tomboyish and did not want to dress up. However, when she arrived, she was Gorgeous. She got dolled up for prom and brought her older brother because he missed his prom. We all sat together at the dinner table, and I was enjoying myself, finally having some fun and feeling relaxed.

After a while, I looked over at Arthur; he had his arms crossed and a disgusted look. I approached him and asked what was wrong, and his response was, "Didn't Dee's brother try to date you in the past?" I responded, "Yes, but that was a while back when we broke up, and he knows I am back with you." I forgot that I had shared that info with Arthur before prom. When I went to get my professional high school photos done, Arthur came with me, and I told him that Dee's brother gave me some money for the pictures to make him a little jealous. That was a big mistake because now it had backfired on me at the prom. Arthur acted like a jerk, walked off the dance floor with me while I was still dancing, and caused such a scene that Dee and her brother left to sit elsewhere. I was so hurt, embarrassed, and devastated. All I wanted was to have my best friend there with me at prom. She always would say, "Why are you still with him and put up with his ways? She would say, "I don't get it; you could be with anyone else. Nobody got time for that!" All I could say at the time was that I loved him, and Dee would ask me what love had to do with it.

After prom, we ended up at my house. Another reason I had to leave prom early was because of the limo service. Because of the crappy night I had, my older sister promised that she would take me out after prom because I did not want to go to the after-party, especially because my best friend was not going. However, when I arrived home, my sister was in bed, saying she had a bad headache. I was disappointed because I could have gone with my best friend. She was going to a nice Reggae party, but I had already told her I was not going because I was hanging out with my big sister; Dee had already left. All Arthur could do was apologize repeatedly as I sat on my porch in my prom dress and cried until about 3 a.m. My prom night was awful.

CHAPTER 3 | COLLEGE LIFE

It was time for my first year in college to begin. I was the first in my immediate family to go to college and graduate from high school, so it was a big deal and somewhat scary. I had no one to tell me anything about college or what to expect. I thought I was not smart enough for college due to being labeled with a learning disability. However, I figured it out with the help of my sister and God. By now, my high school best friend Dee had left. She received a scholarship to a university in a different state, so I had to fend for myself.

I decided to attend a business college in town, but I did not know anyone on the campus. Eventually, I met my next best college friend, Kiki.

Kiki and I both worked downtown while pursuing our degrees. She was fun, energetic, and a social butterfly; Everyone loved her. We did not have driver's licenses, so we would bum rides to the clubs together. We often got rides from one of Kiki's good friends whom she had known since high school; she became my friend also; We ended up forming a little pack, hanging out together since we all had a boyfriend that lasted through high school. We all had been with our boyfriend, trying to make it last and work while in college.

We soon got our licenses and our cars, which made it much easier to hang out. However, I was maturing and becoming more focused. I wanted success, a career, to handle my finances, and to have my own place to live and support myself. Even though my mindset was changing, Arthur was not evolving. He was not training or pushing to accomplish anything; We were going in the opposite direction. I would often convince him to at least put money away for a bus pass so he could continue with his welding classes, get a job, and, most importantly, visit me. I told him I would not be chauffeuring him around or using my car, and if he wanted to see me, he would prove it.

I remember one time I was running late to class and was at his house, so I asked him to drop me off at school; my class was only two hours. I told him that he had better pick me up on time. I said, "Do not be late, I repeat, do not be late, and do not have nobody in my car!" He was about ten minutes late to pick me up, and I was unhappy. There were no cell phones back then, so I tried calling his house from a payphone. I was pacing back and forth, but after a while, he showed up with his friend in my car! He had not listened to a word I had said. Things of this nature were beginning to irritate me big time.

I did not allow Arthur to use my car much after that incident. I would let him run to the store or to get something for his mother, but that was a few times. We did not go out to nice restaurants, dates, plays, or concerts because that would mean I was purchasing. The thing we did most was watch movies and eat fast food. I would make sure he put money away for us to have something to do together besides sit at his house, or as the old folks would say, "laying up."

Despite the bad season, We had our good times, and Arthur made me laugh; he was again very silly and crazy like I was. We could talk about anything, and the physical attraction was phenomenal! I believe that was what made me stay. I was trapped in thinking that giving and having great intimate relations would make our relationship work. The enemy had me believing that was love. We would have intense, intimate getaways some weekends, staying at my sister's house while she was gone, giving us just enough time to playhouse.

By the third semester of college, my classes started getting harder, and I failed a class, which caused me to be placed on probation with my work-study job at the Federal Building. I was so invested in having fun and going out that I was not thinking about my grades as I should have or about my job. I thought the job was boring and not my career; I was foolish for not taking it seriously then. Despite the ups and downs, I had my hustle; I had two jobs at the college. I worked as a lab monitor tech and an office clerk during the evenings. I would run back and forth from my job at the Federal Building in the early mornings and then to classes. I returned to the

Federal Building in the afternoons and then to the college for evening work. I worked hard and had money, but my man did not.

By summer, I ended up with a 60 percent in another class, which was technically not failing, but according to the arrangement of the probation at my job, it was received as failing. Even though I retook the failed course, it lowered my overall grade point average. Therefore, I lost my federal job. Unfortunately, losing my job allowed me to continue playing house that summer. One time, Arthur and I stayed at my sister's apartment for about three to four weeks. My sister was not staying there anymore because she had not paid rent and was avoiding the landlord. The landlord often told me, "Tell your sister I need to see her when you talk to her."

We spent a lot of intimate time together. It was like the movie 9½ Weeks with Mickey Rourke and Kim Basinger; it was wild. If I kept him busy and active, I thought he would not want or need to be with anyone else; I also thought he was my soulmate.

One night while staying at my sister's apartment, Kiki and I, along with the girls, wanted to go out.

I believe Kiki had broken up with her high school boyfriend by now, so we would go out often without our boyfriends. That night, I left my boyfriend at home and told him not to go anywhere or let anyone in because we did not have a key to the apartment.

I went out with the girls, and we had a blast. We drank heavily, so I was pretty wasted. I planned to use the back stairs to bypass the landlord and enter through the back door. It was raining very hard when we were leaving the club. After I was dropped off, I climbed up the back stairs and started knocking, but no one answered. I knocked on the side window, and still no response, even though I could see that the T.V. was on. I was soaking wet by now, so I had to return to the stairs to use the side door. I had to wake the landlord to get into the house. Eventually, the landlord opened the door, and I had to hold a small, awkward conversation and come up with a lie about where my sister was and why I needed to get into the apartment. When I arrived at the top floor of the apartment, the inside door was still locked, and I had no key! I was banging on the door, but no answer. This went on for about an hour. The landlord's dog was in the hallway and came up the stairs to sit with me. We both fell asleep on the floor in front of the door. I was furious, cried, and thought what a fool I was. I began thinking, what if he had someone in there and was too afraid to open the door because there was no other way out? I also wondered whether or not he went out.

Around daylight, I heard walking and a cough, so I banged on the door, and suddenly, he came and opened it. He said, "Hey, you just got here?" When I got in, I grabbed a knife and was about to kill him! He was running from me, but he could hold my wrist. He told me that he had passed out from drinking, and he never heard me at all; He had to talk me down from losing it. Needless to say, that incident ended our "playing house." The red signs were starting to pop up for me everywhere, but I, for some reason, seemed to be color-blind.

CHAPTER 4 | THE SURPRISE

By the beginning of the next school year, I was working at the school in a different part-time position but still looking for something else. Arthur and I were still together, but we were still having periodic fights and spending less time together. One day, I remember him being short on the phone and rushing me to get off. I told him maybe I would come over, and he abruptly responded, "No, it's no need. It is late, and I am tired, so you do not need to come over!" I had been spending the night at his house; his mom had allowed me to stay there, even though it was awkward. He begged me to stay with him numerous times; therefore, his not wanting me to come over sent a big red flag to my brain. I began to think he had someone over his house, and I was determined to find out!

I wore sweatpants and a top, tied my hair in a headband, and wore no earrings because I was preparing to fight. Arthur never hit me or fought back. I was the one who normally did the fighting. Growing up, I saw a lot of fighting in the home, so I thought it was normal.

When Arthur and I first started dating, we argued, and he told me he'd slap me. I threatened him and said, "I'll slap you back." He said I could not beat him, and I told him maybe not, but we would surely be fighting. He playfully pushed me, and I lost my balance and fell. He tried to help me up, but I started swinging and punching him until he grabbed me and held me until I stopped, and then he apologized. Another time, we were leaving a party and had been drinking. I had only been drinking a little because I knew I would be driving, but Arthur wanted to go to another party at his aunt's house. He was driving, which he shouldn't have been because he was almost at the point of being drunk, but I did not know how to get to his aunt's house. I was trying to get him to go home, but he wanted to go back to the party, so we started arguing in the car. I told him to pull over, and he would not; I told him to stop the car, and he would not, so I threw the car in park while driving. He turned the key in the ignition, took it out, and said, "But you don't have the key." I started fighting and hitting him for my keys. Suddenly, we were out of the car in the middle of the street, and he threw my keys. I started hitting him because I was very angry. The next thing I knew, the police pulled up (oh snap, I thought); they put their siren and lights on us, and with a loudspeaker, we were told to put our hands against the car, and two Black female cops came up to us. That was a blessing in disguise; God was looking out for me through it all.

One of the police officers took him to the side, and the other put me in the back of the police car to talk to me and hear what was happening. I told her that I was driving and trying to take him home, but he was fighting because he did not want to go home. She asked if I had been drinking, and I told her I had one small drink. The female police officer told me she would let us go, but we better go straight home. She said the only reason why she placed me in the back of the car and not him was because I was hitting him, and he could have hit me, but he did not. She told me that I looked like the aggressor. I was so scared and glad at the same time. We drove slowly and quietly back to his house.

Reflecting on the night I mentioned earlier.

When I reached his house, I parked on the street so no one would hear me coming. I went to the side door, knocked, and rang the doorbell. Arthur's father came to the door and stared at me momentarily, looking shocked. Then he said my name to make sure it was me he was talking to. I said, "Yes, sir!" He opened the door and told me to wait a minute while he went to get Arthur. This had never happened before, so now, I was suspicious about what was happening, and I had to wait at the door. His father returned and said he was coming. When I heard his dad sit down and start talking to Arthur's mom, I snuck around to Arthur's bedroom door. I listened close to the door First, and I could hear him shuffling and talking, so I tapped on the door a few times without saying a word. He opened the door, and to his surprise, I was standing there! I could see a girl sitting on the bed with her head down, not saying a word, so I started yelling at him and said, "Oh, this is what you are doing? Who is she?" I launched after her, but Arthur grabbed me. By then, I heard his dad saying he was not getting involved, but his mom yelled, "Stop! What are you doing here? Why did you let her in here?"

During the commotion, I was still swinging, and Arthur picked me up, put me in the bathroom down the hall, and closed the door. He was trying to talk to me, but I was not having it. I was still trying to fight him. He ended up swinging at me (I said at me) to knock my glasses off! I do not know why he did that, but all hell broke loose! I started kicking and punching, and he had to grab me from behind to hold me. I managed to turn my head around enough to bite him, and I bit him hard like a dog and would not turn loose.

I do not know how he got the door open or how his mother got in, but I can recall her telling me to turn her son loose and stop biting him. I remember him yelling and saying he was going to start punching me in my head if I did not turn him loose, so eventually, I did.

I started to calm down and realized that I was making myself look like a fool and a crazy person. I never wanted to be in a fighting relationship because I had seen too much of it and did not want any parts of it, especially if one was cheating. It was not worth it!

He eventually told me the girl's name and said she had just arrived and came to see him. I asked him if they were involved, and his responses were slow and confusing, flaring me back up again. However, his mom asked me to leave because I was acting disrespectful. Arthur told her they were leaving, and he told the girl to go down the hall as he held me. The only reason I did not go through him was because his mother was standing there, but I did call her derogatory names as she rushed past, which was wrong because it was not her fault.

I told his mother I was leaving and apologized for disrespecting her home. She asked me if I was going to leave or try to fight her son when he came out. I told her I would be outside her house and not on her property.

When he came outside, I was waiting for him; I do not remember what I said, but I am sure it was some choice words. His mother was yelling, "he is going to beat you, girl; you better go on." I picked up a big stick that was lying on the ground and was taunting, telling him to come on and try it. I started going towards the girl's car to hit it, but my self-consciousness told me not to do it, so I stopped. I was hoping Arthur would have pushed me or tried to hit me as he was going to her car, but he did not. I hurriedly jumped in my car to follow them and see where she lived. The girl took off in her car, and I drove behind them. I wanted to hit the back of her car so badly, but I did not want to tear up my car. We were driving about 70 mph down a two-lane street. I would get up next to them, yelling and swearing, "Pull over." I could have been in an accident several times during this car chase, but thank God for His protection.

Arthur, by now, thought it was funny. He blew kisses and lipped "I love you" out the window. This made me furious. They eventually turned, and I was still going straight, so I had to turn around to go back, and by that time, I could not find them. I was so livid.

After driving around for a while trying to find them, I ended up back at his mother's house. I knocked on the door to ask her if Arthur had returned home. She invited me in and began telling me the truth. She said she told Arthur he needed to tell me, but she would since he had not.

She told me that he had a baby with the girl who was in his room, and the baby was about a month old. She went on to say that he had another daughter by another girl who was going on two years old. At that moment, all I could say was, "Are you for real? Are you kidding?" She said she kept telling Arthur to tell me because it was not right, and it was not her place to tell me, but since he brought the mess to her house, she was telling me because right is right. I was puzzled, shocked, and in a disarray of sorts. I left there and went home.

I was in disbelief; I kept thinking this could not be true. Arthur had told me he loved me, that we would be honest with each other, and that there was no one else he wanted. I thought to myself, how could this have happened? I gave him love, support, and honesty, and I thought we would spend our lives together in happy bliss. I was devastated.

Arthur called that night and said he knew his mother had told me. I asked him if it was true and he told me yes. I was crushed! All I could say was, "I do not believe you." Deep down inside, I wanted this to be a joke, but it was not.

Arthur called the girl and had us on a three-way call so I could hear the truth that he had been hiding from me. I had a silent breakdown, and he began to apologize and plead his case, saying it was an accident and he was drunk. I was not trying to hear it, so I told him it was over and hung up the phone.

I cried myself to sleep, talking to God and asking Him to help me get over Arthur. I asked Him to send me someone true and faithful, someone who would love me and adore me and not want another; someone kind, who loved the Lord, went to church, and wanted to be somebody and do great things. This became my prayer.

As the months passed, Arthur was still calling, trying to get back into a relationship with me. I had been talking to many older ladies to get their views and perspective. Some said I should kick him to the curb because he is no good; if he did it once, he would do it again. Others told me that men are dogs and cheat, and another person said to me that I should be thankful that it was not me. The last comment seemed to strike a nerve inside me. I became confident again and said, "That's right, at least it was not me! I was not the one held down by a baby without help! I reminded myself that I was in college, young, had a good job, money, and car, and could date whomever I chose. I told myself that I was too young to be stressed.

Reflecting on that season of my life, I now realize that I should have been on my face talking to the Lord instead of other people, but at that time, I did not know better.

I started partying, hanging with my girls, dating other guys, and enjoying life, or so I thought. Arthur was still trying to get back in with me, telling me that I was the one for him, that he did not want the other girls, and that he wanted us to try again. I remember a statement that my mother told me about her and my dad when they separated because of my dad's infidelity. She had told him that if he wanted her to take him back, there might be a chance, but she would want to live and experiment, too. This was the ultimatum given to Arthur, basically saying that two can play that game. I stopped hurting, caring, and trying; I was in it to have fun! I told him I did not want to hear anything about his babies or their mothers, and I did not want to be around them; I was choosing to ignore it.

CHAPTER 5 | HEARTBEAT

Amidst this, my grades were slipping; I had already lost the student work program at the Federal Building and was trying to look for other work while finishing my associate degree. I had gotten a job at the Post Office for seasonal hire and hated it. It was stressful for me, and many nights, I would end up staying at Arthur's house because it seemed to relax me and help me sleep. Of course, staying there meant that there were times of intimacy. One night, my college girlfriend threw herself a 21st birthday party, and I invited Arthur to come out with me. We partied all night, with heavy drinking, having a grand ole time until Arthur and I ended up at a hotel. The next week, I was stressing over finals at school, and then I realized I had not taken my birth control pill in the last three days; I freaked out, and now I wanted to pray. Pray? The damage was already done, is what I was telling myself! I took those three pills to catch up and hoped that it prevented the unthinkable.

****

Two months passed, and I started a new job at the Federal Building; I was in my last semester before graduating with my associate degree, and things were starting to look good, or so I believed. After a while, I started feeling sick to my stomach and had stomach pains. I could not figure out what was going on. I told friends, and everyone thought I had a stomach virus, so I scheduled an appointment to see the doctor. At one point, I was even wondering why my breasts were sore; It hurt to the touch, and I still could not figure out what was going on with me.

The Visit To The Doctor's Office

I went in to see the doctor, told her my symptoms, and she asked, when was my last menstrual cycle? I honestly could not remember; my cycles had been abnormal since I had started taking birth control. From what I could remember, it would come in one month, then skip a month or two. I told the doctor that I did not think I was pregnant and that it was probably just a stomach virus. She ordered some blood work, gave me antibiotics, and told me to get some rest.

Two days later, I received a phone call from the doctor's office with a very nice greeting, "Hello, Miss T. We got your lab results back. We have great news; it looks like you are expecting!" I was silent for about 30 seconds, then asked, "Expecting what?" The staff said, "You are going to be a mother; You are having a baby!" She was very excited for me. After another long pause on the line, I begin to question her. I asked her how is this possible while I was on the pill. She told me that it was a chance to get pregnant when on the pill, especially after missing some days, and she told me that we would need to schedule an ultrasound to be able to see how far along I was. I was in total shock and devastated all at the same time. I began to think that I'd become the fool, after all that drama, to end up pregnant by a guy who was not progressing or changing anytime soon! I had goals, visions, and dreams, and he had 40oz weed, nothing but sex on the brain, and we were going in two different directions. I wondered how I would be able to manage a baby; I did not even like changing diapers because my stomach could not take it! I had just decided to continue my education and get a bachelor's degree. I was going to North Carolina to finish school with my best friend; all these thoughts ran through my mind.

I cried for hours and finally knew I had to tell my mother when she got home from work because I did not want to have the ultrasound by myself. I was scared to death and had no clue what an ultrasound was. I knew that I did not want to tell my big sister yet because I was thinking of having an abortion, and I knew she would be totally against it and try to talk me out of it. My sister had tried so hard to have a baby for so long, and finally, she did. She gave birth to my niece just two years earlier, so I did not feel comfortable talking to her about the situation. My best cousin was gone off to the military overseas; therefore, my mom was the only one I could trust to keep me calm.

My mother came home from work, and it was about midnight. She was a nurse assistant and worked from 3 pm-1 am. I called her to the basement because that was where my bedroom was. When I reached 18, I wanted my own apartment or dorm room, so my dad created my studio-like apartment in the basement. My dad wanted me to stay home; he did not want me to leave the house. I had an outer living room set up and a separate bedroom. My mom came down and sat on my bed, and I told her that I needed to tell her something, but she had to promise not to get upset. My mom blatantly asked, "Are you pregnant?" *Talk about having a smooshed face.* I said, "Wow, how did you know?" My mom always would say back then, "I have ESP!" I guess that means extra special powers.

Mom was very happy with the news, yet again, I was shocked. I could not believe or understand why she was so pleased. I had to burst her bubble by telling her that I was thinking of having an abortion. She asked me why, and I explained to her that I could barely take care of myself and that Arthur already had two kids that he did not take care of. I also told her I planned on continuing my schooling after graduating with my lower case Associate's degree. I reminded her that I did not like pain or changing diapers and highlighted the fact that I did not know how to raise a baby.

My mom listened patiently without judgment and said, "Well, I could help you with that, but whatever decision you make, I will support you, and I am here for you." I told her I had to go for an ultrasound to see how far along I was before I could arrange for an abortion due to me not remembering when my last menstrual cycle was, so I needed her to go with me. I told her I did not know what an ultrasound was, but I was scared to death. My mom explained everything, calmed my worries, and agreed to accompany me. At that moment, I asked her to promise that she would not tell anyone, not even Dad.

The visit to the hospital for the ultrasound was a piece of cake, nothing I should have been worried about. When I heard the baby's heartbeat, I was in awe; I could not believe a human life was inside of me, and my mom's eyes were filled with tears. They informed me that I was a little over four weeks pregnant in the first trimester. I told them that I would like to have an abortion, and they scheduled me to see the doctor. I still had not told anyone until a couple of days before meeting with the doctor.

When I went to see the doctor who was going to do the abortion, my mom came with me again but waited in the waiting room during the appointment. The doctor and the nurse started to tell me what the procedure would involve. The doctor spoke of the cutting, sucking, and stopping the heartbeat, and I instantly became lightheaded and nauseous. I kept telling the Dr. and the nurse that I felt like I was going to be sick, but they just looked at me as if I was speaking another language. When I finally started gagging, they grabbed a garbage can and told me to relax and lie down for a while. I had gotten so scared to have the procedure but even more scared to push a baby out. Oh Lord, what was I going to do? I thought. I reminded myself of what needed to be done and that it was the best decision. I remembered my cousin and I making a pack never to have kids.

After a few minutes, I called the doctor and nurse back in and proceeded to schedule the abortion appointment. I was shocked when they said OK and told me to return the following day. I was thinking, "Wait, what, so soon?" They told me to be there at 7 a.m. and not to eat anything after midnight. I came out and told my mother my plans, and she was supportive and said she would come back with me but that I should let Arthur know; I was thinking, "Oh yeah, him."

I had my mom stop by his house before we headed back home, and she waited in the car. Arthur opened the door, but no one else was at home. I told him I had something to say and that he should sit down. He looked worried and kept asking what was wrong; I told him I was pregnant." At first, he kept saying, "Yeah, right, sure you are. Quit lying; what's wrong?" I said, "It is the truth; I am not lying, and you can stop smiling." I told him I just had an ultrasound and heard the heartbeat. I told him my mother was in the car and he could ask her. Arthur went to ask my mother, and she told him that what I said was true.

Arthur came back in, grinning ear to ear, but I had to burst his bubble as well. I had to let him down slowly and inform him of my reasons for not wanting to keep the baby. I reminded him that he already had two children that he could not support, which would mean that I would not have support either, and I could not afford a child by myself.

He seemed slightly saddened but agreed it would probably be the best thing for him now. I told him, "Well, good, because it is scheduled for tomorrow." I said, "The Lord must have known I would change my mind, so he made the appointment quickly." He asked if I wanted him to come with me, and I told him no because my mother would be accompanying me, and the appointment was set for 7 a.m. Arthur was cool with it, but a part of him wanted me to call off the procedure.

The next morning, I was up early. I could barely sleep due to fear of what was going to happen with the procedure, and I was scared to death of needles. I took a shower, prayed for peace and guidance, got dressed, and while waiting for my mother, I opened the refrigerator and saw a little ginger ale left, so I drank a glass. My mother came downstairs and asked, "You did not eat, did you?" I told her no, and off we went to the hospital.

Upon our arrival, we checked in, and I was given some paperwork to fill out. One of the questions asked if I had anything to eat or drink after midnight, and I immediately thought, "Uh oh," and put down that I had a glass of Ginger- Ale that morning. When I returned the paperwork and sat down, the receptionist called me back to the desk and asked if I had something to drink. I told her yes, and she had a nasty attitude. She told me to hold on, went in the back, and returned to let me know that I should not have drunk anything because I was informed not to eat or drink after midnight. She further stated that I had to wait to reschedule the procedure a few hours later because they could not proceed with the procedure due to my drinking. She told me that I could vomit, choke, or even die while–under anesthesia. I had no idea it was that serious.

My mother and I went to sit and wait, and they eventually told us that it might be around noon. As we sat, I started pondering over what was taking place. It was the first in five years that I missed taking my birth control pills. Secondly, the doctors had to give me an ultrasound to see how far along I was, which caused me to not only see the baby but also hear the baby's heartbeat. I had to wait and not go through with the procedure due to my misunderstanding of not having anything to drink after midnight.
I told my mother that I was not sure if I was supposed to go through with the procedure, so she took me for a walk so we could talk and pray about it. As we walked, I told my mom that if I

pray and ask God what to do, He is going to tell me not to get rid of my baby because the Bible says, "Thou shalt not kill," and now that I have seen and heard the heartbeat, I just feel like it is wrong. I told her maybe God allowed me to listen to the heartbeat to change my mind, but if I decided to keep the baby, I would need support as I cannot do it alone. I asked her if she would help support the baby, and she said yes. I asked her how she thought Dad would respond, and she said he would fuss a bit but later calm down because he loves babies and would be happy as a teapot. I said, "Well, I guess it is settled; I am not going through with this, and I guess I am having a baby!" We hugged, returned the pager, and left, going straight to McDonald's because I was starving.

I asked my mother not to tell my father, as I was not ready to discuss it, and she agreed. I asked her to drop me off at Arthur's house so that I could inform him of my decision. When I went inside, I first had Arthur believing that I had gone through with the abortion. He was very nice and compassionate, but I told him shortly after that I could not go through with the abortion as I felt God was leading me not to, and after seeing and hearing the heartbeat, I could not go through with

it. I went on to tell him that I was not asking his permission or expecting anything from him. I told him that if I had to raise the child by myself, then, with God's grace and help, that's what I would do. Of course, he exclaimed, that he would be there for me and we would do it together. I shocked him again by asking if we would get married, and his eyes got as big as pancakes. He did not know how to respond, so he moved nervously and stuttered over his words. He eventually responded and said, "Well, hopefully, eventually. We would have nowhere to live right now, and I do not have a job; I do not have my stuff together right now." I was thinking, "Boy, don't I know it!"
I told Arthur I was kidding and that I was not trying to get married. He would need to be looking for a job to provide support, and maybe we could find a cheap apartment and live together first.

When I returned home, my mother had told my father. I said, "MOM! We said we would wait!" My mother said, "Well, he was going to find out anyway, and I was excited, so I figured I might as well tell him." I had to sit in what felt like the hot seat, a chair in the middle of the living room.

My mother was in the kitchen, and my dad said, "I am disappointed in you. You said you were getting a job at the hospital." I told him I could still get a job at the hospital, and he said he thought I was going back to school for my next-level degree. I reassured him that I could still go back to school after I had the baby. What he said next made me angry. He asked, "You had nothing better to do with your time?" I was thinking, what kind of question is that? So, my response was, "Nope, I sure did not!" Of course, he became furious, but so was I. My mother returned from the kitchen and said, "Well, what is done is done. The baby is a gift, and she will need our help and support." My dad immediately digressed and said, "Well, yes, of course, I am going to love the baby; it is a part of me, and I love you, but do not think I'm going to be sitting around babysitting!" My mother and I laughed and said, "Yeah, like you do for my big sister's baby."

CHAPTER 6 | WAKE UP CALL

The next month, my mother and I planned to announce to the church, which was mostly made up of family members. We had planned it so everyone would know immediately, and I would not have to keep explaining myself. Meanwhile, before this took place, I had taken Arthur to see some possible small one-bedroom apartments. Remember, I had a pretty decent job at the Federal Building, plus I also planned on getting government assistance to help with the medical cost and food. Arthur started acting funny as if he did not want to move in with me. It seemed he was afraid of responsibility and commitment because I kept telling him he had to find a job, and he would consider me nagging him. He would say things like, "I want too much" or "I am high class."

I was talking about a nursery for the baby, pampers, bottles, formula, clothes, shoes, etc. I believe it was starting to sink in that this was happening. He had slacked off on calling me, and I barely saw him. We argued about it, and I told him, "Don't think because I am pregnant that I need you and that I have to sit around and twiddle my thumbs until you decide to show up." I said to him, "Once again, I do not need you to do anything for me that you do not want to do; God will provide everything I need, and you are going to mess around and lose me." Arthur would brush me off, trying to say I was nagging him again; I said, "O.K."

It was a Friday night, and Arthur was nowhere to be found again. My younger cousin Neil told me I needed to return to church or choir rehearsal; I had missed about a month or two. My younger cousin also told me that the church had gotten a new young musician for the youth choir. My cousin believed that the new youth musician was the stepbrother of one of our older cousins, who was also the assistant pastor. I told her that I would come out on Sunday. Remember, my mother and I had planned on telling the church congregation that coming Sunday, announcing my pregnancy. My little cousin also told me she was having a birthday party that Friday night and wanted me to attend. I told her maybe I would come, but I would have to see because, at that time, my car had broken down, and I would have to find a ride.

Luckily, my college best friend Kiki called me that Friday night, and I shared the news with her about me being pregnant, but I told her that I hadn't told anyone else yet. I explained how I was bored without a car and how Arthur seemed to think that I would sit around and do nothing and wait on him, but he was mistaken. I told her that life would go on with or without him.
I then asked Kiki if she would like to go out with me to my little cousin's (at the time, I thought it was her sweet sixteen, but it was her fifteenth birthday party). Kiki agreed to get me out of the house and take me to the party.

When we arrived at the party, we could hear the music playing from outside. As we entered, we saw a nice gathering of people; some were family members, and some were not. When we walked in, a song was playing, and we did a line dance, which is an African American version of country line dancing.

My friend Kiki and I jumped right in and started dancing. I started feeling better and like myself again, without worrying about the future.

Later, I saw someone in the back of the house with a mustache and beard. I got my little cousin who was hosting the birthday party and asked her who that guy was, as he looked too old to be at a young people's party. She replied, "That's the new youth musician I've been telling you about, our cousin Joe's stepbrother!" It surprised me, as I was not expecting him to be there. My other cousin Lyn was also in the back by the kitchen with another older guy, and he was with the guy from church. I was curious, so I walked back there to talk to my cousin Lyn, who had not too long returned from studying abroad in England. Lyn had obtained somewhat of an accent, which we teased her about. We would roll our eyes at her, saying, "Girl, you know you are hood, who you think you are fooling."

Lyn wanted to introduce me to the other guy who came with the musician. When I approached the table, I said, " Hey Lyn, who is this? He was sitting at the table with her, and she said, "Oh, this is Josh," but with her accent, I could not understand her. So, she had to repeat his name twice, and then the guy put his hand out and said, "Hello, I'm Josh." I said, "Oh...It's Josh," messing with my cousin sarcastically but with love. The musician guy approached the table, and Lyn said, "And this is his friend Phil." I said, "Oh, easy name to say, Phil." As I laughed, I asked what they were doing in the kitchen, and my cousin told me that Phil was the DJ for the party. I said, "Oh really?" being surprised again. Phil explained that he was helping out because he had the speakers and many songs, so it was no big deal. My first impression of Phil was that he looked like an overgrown man-boy who was underdressed at a teenage party; I was not interested.

My cousin and I walked from the kitchen and stood in the hallway. She was telling me that she was feeling Josh, that he had pretty colored eyes, but Phil had asked her if she wanted to ride with him back to his house to get some more CDs. I asked what her response was, and she said she had told him no. She thought his request seemed weird since she was not acquainted with him. I told her that maybe he liked her, but she smacked her lips and said she did not think so. Either way, she was not going anywhere with a stranger. We eventually went back to dancing and enjoying our conversation with everyone, then Kiki and I left.

The next day was Saturday, and Arthur called me wanting to talk. I told him I could pick him up after I took my mother to work, and after that, I was going to hang out with one of my other cousins named Shell, who had her own place with her boyfriend, Kevin, and her daughter. She was also pregnant with her second child. I told her that I was pregnant but to keep it on the down low as I would be announcing it at church on Sunday. She had known Arthur since we had been dating and was excited for me. I told Arthur that if he wanted to hang with us, he could, but he would have to attend church on Sunday. He did not like going to church. He thought the duration of time spent at church was too long.

After I told my cousin Shell about my pregnancy, I also told her that I had thought about getting an abortion, but I could not go through with it. I figured I could relate to her, seeing how she had a baby already at a young age, was a single mom, and was doing ok on her own. She was also expecting again, so I figured she could give me some pointers and advice.

Arthur agreed that he would go to church with me. After I dropped my mother off at work, I went to pick him up, and then I picked up my cousin and her boyfriend, and we all went to the park. We walked around the park, tripping out and having a really good time and good conversation. My cousin suggested we keep the party moving, head back to the house, cook, and have some drinks because it was getting late. We all agreed, so we stopped at the store, got some beers and snacks, and returned to her house. We had the music on and hung out on the porch. Later, we heard a couple down the street arguing and cursing; they were getting loud, and someone called the police. We continued having our own good time, and of course, I could not drink, but I am pretty silly without drinking. A song by Prince came on the radio called "Do Me Baby." It was a slow song. I told Arthur to let us dance because it is my favorite song.

We went out in the yard and started slow dancing. My cousin was running back and forth in the house because she was cooking and keeping an eye on her daughter. Arthur picked me up, and my legs wrapped around him as we danced. There is a jester in the song that suggests sounds of intimacy, and I started mimicking the sounds in the music. Arthur commented smartly, saying, "See, that is what got you in this predicament." I took offense to what he said and replied, "Predicament, I got myself into?" He said. "You know what I mean!" while laughing, I laughed and said, "Ha, ha, and that is why it is not yours!"

I know I probably should not have said that, but again, I was offended, and I do have a smart mouth; I believe it's inherited. Arthur was pissed at that comment, and he pushed me off of him, which caused me to fall to the ground. By this time, my cousin was coming back outside on the porch, and when she saw what had happened, she ran to push him back while yelling at him. She reminded him that I was pregnant and that he could not push me the way he did. Meanwhile, I was on the ground, but I was laughing because I thought it was hilarious until reality kicked in that I was pregnant, and he pushed me down. I jumped up in a rage and started cussing him out. I started acting like a lunatic, trying to get to him. My cousin was trying to hold me and block us; she was calling for her boyfriend to come and assist, and he came and pulled Arthur back up on the porch. I ran behind them but grabbed the

40oz beer bottle as I got on the porch and tried to hit Arthur with it. Kevin said, "Wait a minute, don't hit me," so I warned him to move out of the way and threw the bottle at Arthur. Surprisingly, it did not break, and he dodged the bottle.
My cousin was hysterical. She was yelling at us to calm down and reminded me that I was pregnant and did not need this level of stress. She told Arthur that he needed to do better.

We eventually calmed down, but I was so over it by now! I felt like something in me had exploded, making me see things differently! I started to see that I did not want this life. I did not want to bring a child into this kind of lifestyle, and it was obvious that he was not going to change. I realized once again that if I had to do it by myself, I had to trust God and move on. That was the last straw; I was over it!

About 30 minutes later, my cousin and her boyfriend started arguing. Arthur and I were still on the porch while they went inside. We could not understand where the argument came from or why/how it started! Shell was very upset and in tears. She was yelling and cursing, and her boyfriend was sarcastically laughing, trying to brush her off but still making remarks that upset her. It was getting late, and it was almost time to pick up my mother from work. I told Arthur I could take him home, but he still wanted to stay with me.

We managed to calm my cousin and her boyfriend down, and I left to get my mother back from work. When she got in the car, she noticed the tension but was cool. She asked me if I was coming home or staying at Shell, and I told her I was staying as she wanted me to stay with her. I also told her that I was still going to church.

The night was very quiet. Everyone settled down, and there was not much laughing or talking. I slept in her daughter's room, and Arthur accompanied me. I was over our relationship and being together, and I told him I called it quits. I told him to let us stop pretending and go our separate ways. He told me if that's what I wanted to do, then no problem. I told him yes and that it was best. That night, I had silent tears and prayers asking God for strength, help, and to provide for me. I felt every bit of that Mary J. Bilge song "Real Love!" I had been searching for someone to call my own, and I prayed to God to send me someone real, to caress me, and guide me towards all the love my heart can feel. I truly prayed for God to take control. I told Him I was releasing myself to His Will and way.

Early Sunday morning, I woke up early and got dressed. I asked my cousin if she was still going, and she said yes. I started helping her get her daughter ready, then called my mother to tell her not to forget me and that we were going to church. I reminded my mother of what we said we would do at church during the announcements, sharing my pregnancy, and she said yes. Arthur was slow, poking around and dragging. I was not talking to him much, so when my mother got there, he asked her if he could ride with her and be dropped off at his house as he was not attending church. I did not say anything because, at that moment, I did not care.

CHAPTER 7 | THE ANNOUNCEMENT

We dropped Arthur off at his cousin's house, and we said goodbye and nothing else. We arrived at church and sat down, waiting for Church to begin. My little cousin Neil, who had the birthday party, was sitting in front of me; she was happy to see us there because my other cousin Shell had also not been to church in a while. She started whispering and pointing towards the piano, saying, "That's him, that's him, that's the guy." I looked up front, and to my surprise, a handsome man was on the piano! He had on a suit, clean cut, and he was rather attractive. He reminded me of my singer, "Prince," whom I adored! I started sweating and feeling anxious because I knew my mother was about to stand up to announce my pregnancy, and here was this nice, handsome man on the organ/piano.

I thought I might want to holler at him later, but there was no turning back because my mother was going towards the mic. On the inside of my head, I was yelling, "Abort, abort, abort the mission, exit stage left!" (Lol) But She started talking into the mic, saying how much she loves me and how good of a daughter I was. I do not remember everything, but it ended with, "Yes, she is having a baby!" My mom informed the congregation that I just wanted everyone to know that this was my blessing, and she was not ashamed. Of course, my younger cousins, who were in front of me, turned around and stared at me. I had to tell them OK, turnaround now, and that I am grown, with a grin.

Finally, I was able to exhale and breathe. It was finally out, and everyone knew it. I was able to move forward with my decision. With the help of the Lord and my family, I knew everything would be alright.

The church had a special program after service that Sunday, but my mother had to return to work that afternoon. She worked the second shift and told me I could not get her car again that evening, so if I wanted to stay, I would need to call my father to come and pick me up. This was the normal practice if my mother had to work. So, of course, now I wanted to stay because I had my eyes on this new piano player. The youth choir was on the program to sing a few selections; now, I could see how the new guy played.

The program started, and the youth choir did awesome; the new guy played well. When the sermon got ready to begin, we all (teens & young adults) vacated the building, as we would often do when it was an afternoon program. We would go and sit outside until the service was over. I was sitting on the top porch of the church, closer to the church doors. My cousin Shell had stayed inside for the service because she had her daughter, and I think she was asleep. Everyone else who came outside was further down the church's stairs, and we knew to talk quietly. The piano player came out, went down the stairs, and started pacing and fussing; he was talking to one of my male cousins, Parnell. He was venting and talking about a situation that happened, and by now, I was sitting there ear-hustling, trying to figure out what was going on and what he was upset about. From my memory, he was venting about his girlfriend, who was going to have a miscarriage, and he was leaving her. He was saying that he did not want to go back home with her, that he found out that she had a boyfriend up the street, and she was cheating on him, and that it was over! He continued to say, "I just know she lost the baby." I was thinking, "Baby, wow!" So, it was my time to get into their conversation and gather information.

I asked him if he had a girlfriend, and he stopped talking, stared right at me, and said, "Yes." He continued venting to my cousin Parnell, who was a senior in high school. From what I had heard from my other cousins, he and the piano guy had become close and hung out playing video games and riding in his car. Therefore, I had to interrupt again and say, "And your girlfriend is pregnant?" He stopped talking again, looked at me, and said, "Yes." Then, again, he started fussing; I interrupted again and said, "And you both live together?" By now, his nerves were on fire with me for asking so many questions, so he asked, "And who are you?" I told him my name was Stacy." My little cousin Neil said, "This is our big cousin. Remember, she was at my party on Friday." Surprised, he said, "Oh yeah, your mother stood up and made the announcement today!" My heart dropped, and my eyes were big as day as I swallowed, and in my head, I thought,

'Well, whatever, he lives with someone anyway, and she's pregnant!" I was thinking there was probably no chance there anyway. Therefore, I went on and nodded my head and told him yes. He then told me that he and his girlfriend lived together, but not for long. He said he was moving out and returning home to his parent's house the following day. He said he did not feel like going home, so I suggested we go to the movies. Of course, all the younger teens were excited to go to the movies, and Phil agreed. We did not know the times or the names of the movie theatres, so I suggested that we go to my grandmother's house to get the Sunday gleaner and look at the movies. She normally buys the newspaper every Sunday. I persuaded my aunts to allow my younger cousins to come along, as I informed them that I would accompany them and watch out for them. My older cousin Shell was upset because she wanted to go home, so I told her my father would still come to pick her up and my little sister to take them back home because I did not want to go home and deal with Arthur. I asked Phil if he would take me home after the movies, and he agreed.

We discovered that the movie theatre was on the other side of town, close to where I lived, but it was a dollar movie. However, Phil said he did not want to drive and asked me if I had my driver's license. I said, "Yes, of course," even though I was nervous about driving because he had a big car (*a Cutlass Supreme Oldsmobile, T-topped*), and I was used to driving smaller vehicles like a Renault Alliance. I also knew I was not the best driver; I had my share of fender benders in my day. However, I did not mention that to Phil.

We all got into the car; my three younger female cousins and Parnell were all in the back seat, while Phil and I were in the front. It was about a thirty-minute drive to the other side of town, and we arrived there safely and watched the movie, "Don't Tell Mom, The Babysitter is Dead." Everyone paid their way; it was only a dollar, which was great! Phil and I were next to each other and laughed the whole time, with my cousin Parnell on the other side of Phil. I admired his friendship with my cousin Parnell because Parnell and I grew up together; he was like my little brother, and he was my heart. I felt like he was my baby brother. We often laughed and tripped out together in the past before I started college. I thought that if he was getting along with my cousin, we may just be compatible.

After the movie ended, Phil said, "Man, I still don't want to go home!" Again, my younger cousins said, "We don't either!" Phil asked me if I had ever been to this place called "Chagrin Falls?" I said, "No, but it is not that far out, but I cannot drive all the way there." Phil decided to drive, and I suddenly started feeling nervous because I did not know him well, and here we were riding all the way to "TIMBUCTU."

I resorted to telling him not to try anything crazy because I was crazy and carried a switchblade, which I did! He laughed and said, "You do not have to worry." I thought he must be interested in me because why would he want to take this long trip when it was getting dark? It was summertime, so it had to be close to nine O'clock.

When we arrived, it was a beautiful park. It had a small waterfall that I had never seen, and it was romantic. On the other side of the park was a carnival, and we all were excited. We tried to get across the street, as it was a busy intersection, but it was shutting down when we got there because it was a Sunday and the last day.

After a while, I told Phil it was time to get my cousins home, and he agreed but stated that he was hungry. Once again, my younger cousins, with excitement, said, "We hungry too!" Phil said he would stop by a wing shop before he took everyone home, so we stopped and picked up some food. Then, we gradually started dropping my cousins off at their respective homes until Phil and I were the only ones in the car. We had another long thirty-minute drive back to my side of town, and he still had to drive back to his house afterward. We laughed and talked along the way, and once back at my house, we sat in my driveway talking for about two more hours; it had to be around 2 or 3 a.m. I shared with him how I had a long relationship since 10th grade and how I was not at first going to have my baby, but I shared how God moved on my heart, and I decided to keep my baby whether I will be with the guy or not. I told him about the situation that occurred the night before and that I was done and wanted to move on and not be with that person any longer because it was just not a good situation anymore. He shared about his relationship again, the problem that happened the night before, and how he knew that the girl was cheating on him and was not sure if the baby was his. He said that he knew she had a miscarriage and that he was moving out. We talked about school, work, and even handwriting. Yes, I said handwriting. I told him I had sloppy handwriting, and he said that he bet it was not sloppier than his, so he wrote on some paper and handed it to me for me to write on it. I wrote my phone number, and he tore the paper in half, then wrote his number down and gave it to me, and we called it a night. As I went into the house, I was on a cloud. I was like, "Wow, I like this guy," but it will probably not work since I am pregnant!

CHAPTER 8 | THE DATE

The next day was Memorial Day; of course, I slept in. When I got up, I checked the voicemail and found out that Arthur had left a message, but it was very dry, only saying his name. I was thinking whatever, I am over it. My dad had started the preparation for a backyard barbecue, and I had invited one of my girlfriends from high school and work, Niecey; she had come over to hang out and have a barbecue. We talked in my basement, and she shared that she just found out she was pregnant. I went on to tell her that it was over between Arthur and me, and I shared the events that led up to my decision to break up and how I met this new guy who goes to our family church. I told her how we clicked, that he seemed nice, and how I believed he liked me even though I was pregnant. She was impressed and said, "Well, you are glowing and seem happy."

She told me that I should follow my heart, and I asked her if she thought I should invite him over to the barbecue to have something to eat. Niecey said she was not sure but then said, "Why not? It can't hurt."

After she left, I gave Phil a call. The phone rang a few times, and then a female answered; I thought, this must be the girl Phil was complaining about. I did not say anything, so I hung up the phone. After I thought about it, I told myself he said she's the ex-girlfriend, so I called back! I was also curious if Phil had moved out or not. The girl answered the phone again, but I asked for Phil this time, and then she replied, "he's not here. Can I take a message?" I told her, "No, thank you," and hung up. After that, I called the other number that Phil had given me, which was at his parents' house, and his mother answered, but he was not there either. I left his mother a message to let Phil know that I called. Finally, I remembered that Phil told me he helped out and worked with my cousin Joe down at my uncle's auto mechanic shop. I called the shop and asked for Phil. I Remember trying to play it off, to disguise my voice to ask for Phil, because my uncle had answered the phone and said, "he's not here; who's calling?" I was stuck, then I laughed and said it was Stacey, and my uncle said, "OK, Stacey, wait, my niece, Stacey?" I said yes, and he laughed and started teasing me, asking me what I was doing calling Phil. I told him that Phil said that I might be able to catch him down there at the shop. I told my uncle I was being nice and wanted to see if Phil wanted a plate. My uncle said, "Yeah, ok, well, if I see him, I'll tell him."

I did not hear from Phil until later that day when he gave me a callback. He told me that he had been moving out of where he lived with his ex-girlfriend, but now he was back home with his parents. We talked and talked again for hours. I eventually asked him if he could start picking me up on Saturdays to bring me to choir Rehearsal. I figured I could begin to return since I had finished my schooling, and I was also ending my job due to budget cuts and layoffs. My car had also broken down, so I was out of a vehicle for a while. I wanted to test him to see if he would commit to seeing me every Saturday, and Phil came through.

He started picking me up for rehearsal, and I admired his desire to be at church and how he could play the keyboard and sing. My older cousin Ann was the youth choir director, and she was cutthroat! She would chew you up and spit you out if you did not have your harmony together, but I loved her so much; I loved her dedication; it was a great choir. Phil, of course, had become familiar with and close to many of my family members. Remember, before meeting me, Phil and Ann were hanging out with his ex-girlfriend and the whole choir, basically my whole family. Their relationship went on for several weeks before Phil met me.

As time went on, Phil and I were becoming closer. Phil had mentioned that he had never been treated or asked out on a date; he said that he was always doing the asking and paying. I told him, well, I loved that a man would even do such a thing as to treat a woman on dates. After he shared this, I thought I would also love to treat my man. Eventually, I set a date and asked Phil if he would accompany me. He was ecstatic. I had little money because I was no longer working, but I told him we would have dinner and a movie date.

We went to Pizza Hut, and I ordered two small personal pan pizzas and two drinks.

I figured that way he could get whatever kind of pizza he wanted, and seeing how I was a picky eater and only liked a meat lover pizza, this way we could have our own. After we ate and talked, I took him to a nicer, fancier-dollar movie that was way up in the suburbs. We got a small popcorn and two small drinks. The whole date cost me roughly around $30, but that was what I could afford, and he loved it! He said that was the best date and best thing any female friend had done for him and that he was truly grateful.

So, we started dating and have been hanging out since that first night in the car. One particular weekend, my cousin, whom Phil called stepbrother, was going out of town, and he asked Phil to stay at his house. Of course, Phil asked me if I would accompany him, but I was hesitant, seeing how close my cousin's house was to my other family members' house. I figured, well, I'm already pregnant, so I don't have to worry about that, and if I wear shades and a big hat, hopefully, I won't get recognized by my family.
I disguised and went to stay for a night with Phil. We kissed passionately; it was like I had known him forever. I was so comfortable as he took me to lie down; he was gentle and kind. We made

love, and it was magical. Our relationship was new, and Phil hung out with me daily. You might wonder, well, what about Arthur? I told him he was free and that the best thing he could do for me was to let me go because we were no longer working. Arthur granted my request and stayed away except for an occasional phone call.

One day, when Phil was dropping me off at home after taking me to get my hair done, and I was craving breakfast in the afternoon, Phil took me to Woolworth's diner for French Toast sticks, sausage, and eggs. We noticed Arthur sitting on my porch when we got to my house and got out of the car. Phil said, "I will let you talk, and I will see you later. I told him he did not have to leave, but he just said he'd see me later, and he jumped in his car and sped off. Arthur tried to joke on him by saying, "That's your skinny dude?" I was like, "Whatever, where is your ride?" As to say, he did not even have a car, so don't clown!

We went into the house because I wanted to eat my food, and as we sat in the kitchen, Arthur tried to make me feel low like I was a "Gold-digger!" He said, "So this dude took you to get your hair done, giving you rides, and buying you breakfast and stuff?" I said, "Well, somebody knows how to treat me; you jealous?" Even though, in reality, I paid for my hair, I would not give Arthur the satisfaction of knowing the truth. Arthur looked and saw I was wearing the watch he had bought me about a year earlier; the watch that I made him buy me because I was mad and felt like he never did anything for me. I had picked it out, made him put it on layaway, and made sure he made the payments; it was only a $60 watch. Arthur thought he could hurt me by asking for it back, saying, "If I bought this, then it is mine; you do not need it; tell that other dude to get you one!" I got so mad and disgusted that I took it off and threw it at him, then I told him he could go; there was no point in visiting me, and he left.

Later, I told Phil all about the visit when he called, and the next day, Phil brought me a Gucci bangle watch with changing color round faces; I could not believe he had done that! I was so shocked and ecstatic at the same time. I was thinking, man, he likes to give, but he also liked to brag at the same time, but at least I did not have to twist his arm to be gracious and provide or twist his arm to put money down for him to purchase it for me. It was a change from the previous relationship.

CHAPTER 9 | THE COURTING

I must mention that during our courting, Phil had been coming over to my house to drop me off, and one night, my dad caught a glimpse of him and asked if that was Phil, Bee's son. I said to my dad, "Who is Bee?" My dad responded, "Bee, your mom's uncle who was married to her aunt (Bobbie). I told him I did not know; I thought he was Joe's stepbrother. My dad had said, "Right, Bee is the stepdad"! Now I was so confused! My family's bloodline is so complicated on my mother's side. I wanted to make sure we were not related, and by now, both Phil and I had to get it clear that the relations between our families were by marriage but not by blood. Whew, that would have been awful.

The time came for my graduation. I was graduating with my associate degree and was so happy and proud of myself.

I planned to graduate with my lower case associate degree and continue pursuing my bachelor's either at the University my best friend attended or continue working towards my BA degree. I had a plan, but I was pregnant now, so my plan was on pause. Nevertheless, I was excited to walk across the stage and be the first in my home to receive a college degree. I was torn because I wanted to invite Phil, but at the same time, I wanted to allow Arthur to attend since he was involved in my life throughout high school and my two and a half years of college. Therefore, I had to explain that to Phil, and he was disappointed, but he understood and said he would come to my house to visit me after graduation. I had asked Arthur to come as well as my family, but of course, once again, Arthur could not make it, so I had an extra ticket that I was going to give to Phil; however, my older sister was nagging that she wanted her boyfriend to attend, and since he had helped me out during my high school prom, I felt obligated for him to attend.

My sister's boyfriend did not attend my graduation; it was disappointing! However, when I returned home, Phil was there to meet me, and he bought me a 14K Herringbone necklace. That was the sweetest thing ever!

A few days later, I went to Phil's house. I had not been around his dad often because he worked a lot; He had two jobs. However, he was at home on this particular day. Phil's father was so excited! He had a clipping that he had cut out of the newspaper of all the graduates from the University where I graduated, and he circled my name to show that I graduated with my associate degree. I thought that was the most precious thing ever; he was so proud of me and told me my degree was an accomplishment. He was very much into school; he held two bachelor's degrees when I met him and later got a Master's in Pastoral Theology.   Phil's mom was an elementary school teacher, but when I met her, she was an Administrator at the Community College.

*****

As time progressed, Phil and I started admiring each other a lot; I was deeply impressed with his demeanor, personality, and heart. He was very kindhearted. There was one thing I did not like about him: his bragging and showing off.

I told him he does not have to talk about what he will do or say so much but to prove it and do it. We would have disagreements, and we were very stubborn and would not back down from any argument. My cousin Parnell thought there was no way we would make it as a couple because we argued so much, but we were not really arguing; we just had different opinions and disagreed on each other's thoughts. What my cousin did not realize was that this allowed us to understand each other more and more. It was a form of communication that needed to be structured correctly. Even though we were both stubborn and bullheaded, we never wanted to leave each other's side. Every day, Phil was at my house, and I was over at his house because we enjoyed each other's company. I loved his mom, and she loved and adored me. One day, we were at his house, and his mother asked if anyone wanted watermelon; everyone replied no, except me. His mother set my plate on the table in the kitchen, and when I went to the kitchen and sat down to eat, Phil came with a fork, trying to eat some of my watermelon. I said, "No, sir! You said no, so you cannot have my watermelon!" He got so mad at me that he grumbled and mumbled, and it was as if he was spitting fire. His mother said, "Son, I could cut you a piece of watermelon," but he kept saying, "No, it's OK if she does not want to share;" I told Mrs. Johnson that he would be ok and that no one was going to put up with his temper tantrum. She laughed hard, tapped me on the shoulder, and said, "I really like you; you know how to handle him." I winked my eyes and then finished my watermelon. Phil rolled his eyes at me, but he was fine.

On another occasion, we were supposed to meet some friends downtown for a jazz festival. Phil came to pick me up at my house. I was waiting on the phone call from my friend Kiki so we could follow them downtown. I stepped out on the porch, and when I returned to my house, Phil had gone into my refrigerator and had gotten a cup to pour a glass of water. I started yelling and fussing at him. I said, "How rude of you; you do not go in peoples' refrigerators when you are a guest. You are supposed to ask. You do not have any manners!" Shortly after, I ran across the street to give my best friend Cece something, and I heard my phone ringing at my house, so I started running back. Phil was sitting by the phone, so I asked why he had not answered. He told me I yelled at him about getting a glass of water so he would not touch my phone. He got me, but I was furious! We got into the biggest argument because he knew I was waiting on the phone call from Kiki! During those times, there were not any cell phones, so I had no way of getting in touch with my girl Kiki. We were all planning on meeting her and her boyfriend downtown. Needless to say, after the arguing, we jumped in his car and headed downtown and ended up having a good time but not with my girl Kiki; we never found them. Those were the arguments we had in our beginning stages of learning one another.

My best cousin in the whole world, Marie, came home from overseas. She had joined the military and recently got married while overseas. She brought her new hubby home for everyone to meet, especially me. We needed to like each other's guy because we were close. I also wanted her to meet Phil. She was impressed with him and could not believe I was finally going to leave Arthur, but she also could not believe Phil was serious about a relationship with someone pregnant!

We all planned on hanging out, showing my best cousin's new husband around the town that Friday night, and going to an amusement park on Saturday. When Friday came, Phil had classes early, so I just hung out with my cousin and her spouse. Every time we would stop back at her place or some relative's house, I would give Phil a call. (*remember, no cell phones*) I was trying to catch him at home, but he was trying to ride around and catch up with us, so we kept missing each other. This continued until late that evening before I finally caught up with Phil back at his house. Phil was furious with me; He thought I was intentionally dodging him. I had to beg him to come down to my aunt's house to see me that night so that I could explain what happened. When he arrived, he parked his car, and then we started arguing about who was supposed to be where and how we kept missing each other. In my head, I started thinking, well, I need to shut him up and fix this quickly because he is supposed to pay for us to go to the amusement park on Saturday, and I wanted to go; I wanted it to be a romantic getaway for us.

I started thinking of ways to end the argument, so I approached Phil and said, "I apologize. You are right; I was wrong and should have stayed in one place and waited for you. Please forgive me." All the while, I was giving him those puppy dog eyes, pulling on his shirt, rubbing on his arms, and trying to get a kiss. Phil tried to play hard, saying, "No, it's not going to be that easy," but I kept pushing back, and then I whispered in his ear and said, "I'll make it right"! He was no longer angry and quite happy and satisfied with me! Therefore, we planned on going to the amusement park the next day. This is how much we enjoyed each other 's company. Even in the worst argument, we still wanted to be around each other; we cared for one another. He made me laugh and made me happy. He treated me like there was no other person more important than me.

****

We held hands at that amusement park and shared cotton candy. He also won me a stuffed animal. We rode the rides—well, the ones I could ride anyway—and had a fantastic day. My Best cousin said she liked him, and he seemed like a good guy, but she could tell he was a bragger.

A few days later, she left and went back overseas. As time passed, it was now time to find out the sex of the baby! Back then, we did not have any gender reveal parties like they do today. My mother went with me for the special reveal. At the ultrasound, the nurse said it was a girl because she had spread open so that we could know for sure. My mom had teared up, so I asked her what was wrong, and she said she was hoping for a boy because she did not have a son and she already had a granddaughter. She went on to say that she was also very happy. I had a lot of assistance from my big sister since she had a baby two years prior. She gave me the book (*What to Expect When Expecting*) and ensured I was reading it. My sister told me I had to take Lamaze classes to help me with breathing since I said I wanted to have a natural delivery. She also made sure I had all my healthy checkups and ate better. Phil wanted to accompany me to my classes, so he and my sister came with me; it was precious. Phil even went to a few of my doctor's visits. It was a little awkward because they called him the dad, and we both would say, "He is not the dad." I remember once when Arthur came to a doctor's appointment with me because I remember saying that this was the father, but I do not remember much else. For the most part, it was just Phil, my sister, or my mother who was with me for support.

CHAPTER 10 | THE PARTY

The time came for my 21st birthday! I am a bit Giddy for birthdays; I always enjoy celebrating my birthday. My mother raised us this way: to be excited for a birthday, instill memories, have parties, or plan something special.

I planned a party at a nightclub near my home and had invitations made; I had the VIP booth, decorations, and a birthday cake and was excited about it! A lot of my family and friends from college were there. We had a blast! My man was there, Phil, of course; he had this big box he gave me for my birthday. All eyes were on me, of course, to open it! When I opened it and looked inside, it was a big purse! A navy-blue leather handbag that was a name-brand bag by Coach. I never had name-brand purses, shoes, clothing, or anything else, but I also did not care about name brands; however, it was still very exciting and impressive. (*I still have that same purse today, and it's still in good condition*).

Phil was a sweetheart, and he enjoyed spending time with me. Whenever I went out, he was there with me, even if it was all girls. I admired that about him: he enjoyed my company, hanging around my friends, and being a gentleman.

We had gone to another party gathering that my girlfriends and sister would visit frequently. It was a hotel's happy hour, and they would provide free drinks for ladies before 8 pm. Phil, once again, came with me. At the club, I had a drink that I gave to him, and then I got another drink. The waiter came over to the table, tried to make a scene, and said, "It's free drinks for the ladies only," and that he needed to pay for his drink. Being a showoff and bragger, Phil asked how much for a bottle. He ended up getting a bottle for our table! When I say he impressed me, he really did, not just me but everybody there.

That was not the only time that Phil impressed me. I bought a VCR for myself when VCRs first came out; they were on the high-expense side, and not everyone had one. Sometimes, I would visit my cousin Shell, and since she didn't have a VCR, I would take mine to her house to watch movies. My VCR ended up not working, and Shell said that her boyfriend could fix it, so I gave the VCR to him in the hopes of fixing it. Weeks had gone by, and it was still not fixed. I went by their house, and no VCR was working or ready for return. It was all in parts, but they kept saying it would be fixed.

I was upset because I did not have a VCR. I should have known they wouldn't be able to fix it! Around the same time frame, my college friend Kiki was having a get-together in her backyard. Phil and I went to her get-together, hung out, and had a good time. I remembered that I had brought the coach purse that Phil purchased for my birthday, and I could not find it when it was time to leave. When I returned home, I searched but could not find it anywhere. I called my friend Kiki to ask her to look around for it, and she could not find it! I believed someone had taken it, and I cried and told Phil how sorry I was for losing something so expensive. Well, guess what? Without my knowledge, Phil bought me a new VCR and Coach purse, not one, but two. I was amazed! I could not believe he had done that for me. That same day, I found my purse. I drove in my mom's car, and I had forgotten I left it in the back seat on the floor. I had to call and apologize to my friend Kiki for the confusion. I told Phil he had to return the new purses and that it was too much to keep three! He was upset and did not want to return the purses, but I told him I could not accept or expect him to spend that money on them. Eventually, I had him return the purses. I originally told him to return the VCR also, but he told me no because it was something for both of us. I wondered what he meant, but I didn't bother to ask.

These were the kinds of things that Phil demonstrated to me to let me know he would be there for me, and in my eyes, he was the one. He showed that he genuinely cared about my well-being, concerns, and what was important to me. He demonstrated that he was willing to be there for and support me.

As it got closer to my delivery, Phil told me that most of the money he was using was money he had inherited after the passing of his grandfather. He told me how it was depleting. Therefore, he took on a part-time job at Pizza Hut. He said he wanted to help with anything needed for the baby. I mean, who could have seen this coming?

A man would come into my life and take on the role and responsibility of a father when he could have just walked away; he was not obligated to me. We were not married! This type of love is what I prayed for. When Phil finished his shift, he would come to my house to count his tip money and give me half his tips. I needed to purchase a crib and a playpen, and I wanted a certain type that was more expensive than the others. The one I wanted had a changing table that turned into an infant crib and was foldable to carry wherever needed. I also needed wallpaper to change the outlook of my bedroom for my newborn. Phil agreed to help me with all of this.

I needed space in my bedroom, which was in the basement, for me and the baby. My dad had built a makeshift closet for me in my room, so where that closet was located, my dad decided to tear it down for space for the crib, and he would build another one for me on the outer part of the bedroom. Phil got along very well with my dad; they always hung out, and he went with my dad to purchase the materials for the new closet. Phil told me that my dad said to him that he was a great man and that he respected him. He told him he was doing everything a father should do when it was not his responsibility. My dad was proud of him for that.

CHAPTER 11 | THE DELIVERY

It was finally time for the delivery! My delivery date was close to the beginning of December; it was the weekend after Thanksgiving, and I was ready to have this baby. In my mind, this baby was coming now! In the past, we usually went out on the weekend after Thanksgiving, so I got with my older sister and asked if Phil and I could hang out with her. We went out Friday night and stayed out all night long, dancing the night away into Saturday morning. I did not get home until about 6:30 am. When I got home, I felt wet, so I changed my clothes, went to bed and fell asleep. When I woke up, I wasn't sure if my water broke because it wasn't a lot of water; I was just wet as if I were sneezing, and a little water came out. Since it wasn't a lot of water, and I was unsure, I ignored it. After a little while, my stomach started cramping, but just a little bit; however, I was thinking, yeah, this could be it now, that maybe it's time to have this baby!

Phil had to work that Saturday afternoon; I told him how I was feeling and might be going into labor later, so he asked me if I wanted him to stay home. I told him no, it would be a while before I would go to the hospital, so he should go to work. As the day went on, I kept having contractions. They said you should walk, so I felt like walking in the mall. I called my BFF girlfriend Cece across the street to see if they were going to the mall for the holiday shopping, and she said they were. I walked around with Cece and her mom and told them that I thought I might be going into labor, but I knew it would be a while, so I just wanted to walk around.

We started walking around the mall for maybe an hour and a half. The contractions started getting closer, so I had to sit down. When I got back home, I told my big sister that I was going into labor that night. I had to wait for my mother to leave work, so Phil came over. He helped me count how long it was between the contractions. He would talk to me to keep me distracted during the contractions. I also spoke with a few people on the phone to deflect the situation until I

couldn't talk on the phone anymore due to the pain. I wanted to take a hot bath to help ease some of the contractions, which seemed to help for a little while. It had to be about 1 am.
After my mother arrived home, everyone else went to sleep. When I could not take the pain anymore, I told them that it was time to head to the hospital.

I rode in the backseat with my older sister, and my mother drove while Phil followed us. When we got to the hospital, they put me in a wheelchair to take me up to the room and asked me if I was planning on delivering naturally. I said yes because I did not want any drugs. Once settled in my room, I had my mom, older sister, and Phil beside me. Everyone was taking turns and rubbing my back, which seemed to hurt most. I was tossing and turning, moaning and groaning. They said I had dilated to 3cm and asked me when I noticed the water leak that happened earlier that morning, and I told them I was not sure if that was my water breaking or not. As time went by, I kept having contractions, but I did not dilate much more. The Dr. decided to break the remaining part of the sac to speed up the process, but it just kept hurting to the point where I yelled out and said, "Can you guys please give me something?" The nurse said, "You said that you did not want any drugs; you wanted to do this naturally!" I hollered, "Not Anymore! May I please have something for his pain?"

They prepared me for the epidural. When they were giving me the shot in my back, I was having a contraction, but I still sat very still without moving and took that shot. It was funny later; my sister had drawn a comic strip of when I first came into the hospital with a smile, then how I went to a frown and then to a mad face demanding drugs, and finally went back to smiling. It was a silly and funny but true drawing.

After the epidural, I was relaxed and waiting for that urge to push. By now, we were fully into Sunday; Phil had to leave because he had to play at church but said he'd be back after church. When he came back, I still hadn't pushed any baby out. My regular doctor was not on call that weekend, so I had different doctors who kept checking on me.

Monday morning, around 1 am, my doctor arrived. He was upset and said they should have given me a C-section because the baby had turned sideways, and we needed to get her out now. I felt scared and started shaking as if I was freezing! I started chattering my lips, and I could not stop. I was biting down on my tongue due to the chatter, and I asked my sister to come with me to the surgery room because she had also delivered my niece by C-section. I felt that she would be able to calm my nerves and keep me at peace. When we got to the delivery room, the staff strapped my arms down, and I started shaking even more frantically! I was asking if I could have a tongue dispenser or something to hold my tongue down because I could not stop biting it from all the chattering of my teeth, but no one was listening to me, probably because I was not speaking clearly. My sister was so amazed at the procedure that she was not listening to me, but she told me everything that was happening. She told me when I was about to be cut, she told me she could see my insides, and then told me she could see the baby!

I could feel them pulling the baby out, and once she was out, my sister said, "There she is, OK-

OK, we need to hear you cry, baby." I was still chattering, trying to say, "What's wrong? What's wrong!" Again, no one would say anything to me. Then finally, my sister said, "They needed to do a little more pop on the butt, and my baby girl began to cry. It was the best noise I had ever heard! They began cleaning her off, and my sister said, "Oh my gosh, she is so beautiful. She has sandy blond hair." Then we both heard the nurses say, "She has blue eyes!" All my tears, all my fears, the shaking, and the chattering ceased! I was overwhelmed with happiness, and I started crying.

They came and laid my baby on my chest, and she was just as beautiful as they had described! She was looking at me with those deep blue eyes! I told my sister to watch my baby as they finished cleaning her off and getting her ready; I said, "Please watch my baby's bracelet on her arm, so I will know they did not try to switch my baby."

When we returned to the recovery area, seeing my mom's face and Phil's face looking relieved, knowing that we both made it and were OK, was priceless. When Phil saw the baby, he told me she was the most beautiful thing he had ever seen, that she stole his heart right out of his chest, and that he loved her. My sister ruined the moment when she blurted out, "Aren't you going to call Arthur?" I told her I was not planning on it because he had not checked on me, but she insisted, and I told her I would call him and let him know.

Eventually, we borrowed a phone from the nurse, and I called and told Arthur that I had the baby and was at the hospital. He said he did not have a ride and asked if someone could pick him up. I told him no one was available to pick him up, and if he wanted to see the baby, he would have to figure it out like he does everything else, and I hung up the phone.

Finally, everyone was able to go home and get some rest. Later that day, I found out that I had an-infection due to all the checking to see if I had dilated; therefore, I had to stay in the hospital longer.

****

The time came for me to name my baby. I thought I would surprise my mother and give my baby her name; however, when I showed her, she said abruptly, "No, name her Sharayle." The nurse brought my baby into the room, and there she was, beautiful as the sun, bright as the morning star, named after her grandmother, with a name meaning royal and crown, the Lord blessed!

Arthur eventually made it up to the hospital about two days later. When he arrived, I was knocked out and feeling very weak. I had not started walking yet, and I had a colostomy bag on because I was not going to the bathroom on my own yet, and no one else was there when he came. I hit the button to have the nurse bring my daughter into the room, and Arthur held her and smiled. For a while, we were silent, but I got a chance to snap a photo. I wanted memorable moments of the whole experience, so I took pictures of everyone who came to see me. My mom came back into the room and started talking to Arthur. I believe I fell asleep because I don't remember anything. When I woke up, he was leaving. I had many other visitors who came to see me and my daughter at the hospital, but Arthur never came back, nor did anyone from his family. However, Phil's family came to visit me in the hospital, and they brought outfits, a case of pampers, and a case of formula.

CHAPTER 12 | THE RETURN HOME

Once I returned home, a new life had started. I had to learn how to be a mother. I thought it would be a piece of cake since I did a lot of babysitting, but it was different from taking care of your newborn baby. I had frightened myself many times while holding my baby and checking on her while she was asleep. I freaked myself out the first time I wanted to wash her hair! I was afraid that I would get water in her face and hurt her in some way. There was so much going through my mind that I ended up needing my mother a lot, and I'm so appreciative that the first two weeks, my mother stayed home from her job to help me out.

The first month of us being home, a few nights a week, my mother would take my daughter upstairs to her room at night so that I could get some sleep. My mother was my rock and gem, and I don't know if I could have gotten by without her help. I am so grateful for her. Phil was also coming by to see me almost every day. He would spend much time at my house, sometimes just sitting upstairs in the living room with my dad. He would ask me what I needed from upstairs in the kitchen and bring me what I needed. I would tease him and say you only use me for my cable TV.

Almost a month had passed, and it was time for New Year's Eve, and I could finally get out of the house. My grandmother was a stickler about not leaving the house until after your first month so that you do not catch pneumonia; it was a traditional rule. However, I had to leave the house about three weeks after my baby was born due to an infestation that had happened in my home. We needed to exterminate the house, so my uncle allowed me to stay at his apartment over the weekend. I invited Phil to stay at the apartment with me. I thought it would be fun and figured it would be as if we had our apartment. I also wanted to see how he would handle a newborn baby through the night. He came over and was very supportive, but my daughter was

hungry when it hit about 3 am and would not stop crying until the bottle was ready! Phil said, "I will have to go home because I need to get some sleep. I have to work tomorrow."
He left and returned the next day but did not stay overnight. Phil might have been tripping a little bit also because I told him there would be no hanky-panky until my six-week checkup. I thought to myself how badly he failed that test, but at the same time, I thought it was funny. At least he tried and was there. I knew and understood that he did not have any younger siblings, nieces, or cousins, and he did not babysit, so he did not know the cost or the duty of having a newborn baby in the home.

Coming back to New Year's Eve, Phil wanted to take me out, so he planned a nice romantic evening for us. My parents babysat for me. He booked a fancy hotel during that time, it was fancy, and we also went out to dinner. I reminded him that I still had to wait another two weeks before intercourse and that this was what the doctor recommended. The first night we were at the hotel, we enjoyed our time together; we semi-crashed a New Year's Eve party, danced in our room, gave each other a toast, and then went to bed without any relations. I reminded Phil again that I had to wait; his reply was, "OK, I understand."

Early the next morning, I woke up and was so impressed. I adored the fact that Phil had ordered room service for breakfast. I thought, wow, I love this guy; he is so sweet to me and willing to wait and not make a big deal out of anything. I thought about how we had such a lovely night that I could not ask for a better boyfriend! So then, of course, I had to start messing with him, kissing him, loving on him, and things took their course, and then Phil was a happy camper!

As weeks passed, we were with each other almost every day, and he stayed late at my house until after 1 am. It was to the point that one night, my mother asked, "Does he have to be here every night that I get home?" My mother worked the second shift and would get home around 12:30 am every night. She would visit the basement where I slept to see her grandbaby. She felt like she had to look into Phil's face every night, and I guess it was starting to get on her nerves. I also felt overwhelmed because I was trying to entertain him, learn how to be a new mom, and figure out the next move in my life.

One day, when Phil came over, we were staring in the crib looking at my daughter, and I asked him what his thoughts were about us being together as a family and making a real commitment. I said, "Life is short; we should settle down, get married, raise a family and be happy." I asked him what he thought about getting married or moving in together, and he laughed shyly and thought I was joking. He then said it was too soon for that, and we needed to plan things to be established before we could do all that, especially financially. Therefore, the thought was brushed off.

******

Arthur had not visited or even called, so I called him one night. I was feeling pretty down. I believe I was in some postpartum depression stage. I just wanted to know why. Why, after all the years we had been together, of us becoming very close friends, spending so much time together, that he told me we were best friends, now to drop me like a hot potato without concern. Not to mention that I just had his baby! When I got him on the phone, I remember sobbing and crying, trying to get answers as to why he would treat me that way and why he did not care. I wanted to know if he ever loved me. I do not remember his answers, but I know I asked about his first baby's mother, if he loved her more than me, and if that was why he never told me about her and having a baby. He responded that he loved her more at first, that she was very important to him, and that he was mad that she moved away, but then he and I had gotten closer together. He mentioned that he was initially involved in the child's life, but in some ways, it stopped. There were no real firm answers to why I was treated that way.

Perhaps a week or two later, Arthur showed up at my house, drunk, saying he wanted to see Sharayle, and then he asked to use my phone. He ended up calling some chick! He was laughing and talking with this girl on my phone! I asked him if she knew that he had children and that he was at my house at that moment. The girl on the phone started yelling and swearing, calling me out my name and asking why I was talking. She said, "Tell her I do not give a blank, blank about who she is and what she has!" I was upset. I said, "Who is she calling names? And you just going to let her call me one?" He laughed and said,

"Well, if the shoe fits." I told him whatever and that they deserved to be together. I further told him he needed to leave my house, and he left.

As time passed, my baby was soon to be three months, but again, I had postpartum depression and was feeling very overwhelmed. I told Phil that perhaps–we should pull back from seeing each other daily. I told him that maybe we needed to give each other some space so that I could concentrate on my baby and get some things done that I needed to do. Phil was upset about what I said; he did not like it and asked me if I wanted to get back with Arthur. I told him no; I did not want to get back with him; I needed a little space."

Phil took what I said differently. One evening, he came to my house and told me we should see other people. I was shocked and asked him why he would say that. He told me that I said I needed space and time apart to think and get things together, so he felt that maybe we should break up and see other people. I told him I did not say I wanted to break up and did not want to be with anyone else. I asked him, "How are you saying we should see other people when you just told me you love me?" I was semi-yelling by this

time, and Phil was trying to calm me down. He asked me why I was upset and thought this was what I wanted. I kept saying repeatedly, "That is not what I wanted"! He explained that he wanted to sow his oats, to see what else was out there before he made any commitment, and suggested that I should do the same! "REALLY!"
I said, "Do whatever you are going to do; you can leave now." I was wondering if that was what guys did: play games with people's feelings and emotions. Here I go again, in this situation! Phil said, "Well, I have a picture of her; you want to see her?" I could have jumped up, uppercut him, then kicked him through a wall! I said, "So, you already got with someone else?" He said, "Yes, she went to my church and is home from college." I was blown away; I did not know what to say, and I could not believe he was standing here asking me if I wanted to see a picture! He thought she was so cute and wanted to show off again and brag. I looked at the picture and said, "OK, whatever"! This dude says, "You see she has long hair"? I am sure I cussed and said, "I don't care"! I kept telling him he could leave now, and he wanted a hug. I was wondering if he was crazy or something.

I believe Phil thought I was trying to hurt him, so he was trying to hurt me, too — immaturity at its best.

I told him I did not want to hug him and told him to go be with his new girlfriend!" Phil persisted, and I finally got up and hugged him, which made me upset with tears. I asked why again. How could he say he loved me yet stand here and break up with me?

The next thing I remember was my doorbell ringing; Phil asked me if I was expecting company. I told him no, I was not expecting company! The doorbell continued to ring, and no one else was home but my little sister, who was upstairs on the second floor, so I said to Phil, "Well, come on, so I can let you out and answer the door." When I got upstairs and opened the door to my SUPRISE, Arthur was standing at my door! We all stood there staring at each other for what would seem like 15 minutes, but it was probably only five seconds. I couldn't believe he was there. I hadn't seen him or heard from him in a month. At that time, the only thing I could muster was, "She's downstairs in the basement. You can go down there to see her" (I was talking about my baby).

Phil hugged me again and said, "Well, I'll see you around, maybe at your church." He said, "I may invite her (the chick) to come." I said, "Whatever, goodbye," and closed the door!

When I got downstairs to the basement, Arthur was in my bedroom looking at the baby sleeping in her crib. We both walked out into the living room and sat on the couch. Arthur immediately knew something was wrong with me; he could tell by the look on my face. He asked what was wrong, and I asked him why he came. He said, "What do you mean? I came here to see Sharayle and you." I said, You did not call me, and I haven't heard from you in a month. Why tonight"? He said, "I was in the neighborhood."

We sat quietly for a few minutes. The TV was playing, and I just started crying silently to myself. I really could not believe this was happening! Here is the guy that I thought I would spend the rest of my life with when I was younger, and it turned out that he didn't want me; then I met a nicer guy who came into my life to be a part of my child's life, and then he breaks up with me out of nowhere! Why was this happening to me?

My baby sister was coming down the stairs to check on me, and I didn't want her to know I was upset, so I jumped up and went into the bedroom, got myself together, and then asked her whether she would sit down in the basement for a minute while I took a walk. Arthur and I went outside and started walking. He said, "So, will you tell me what's wrong?" I said, "Phil just broke up with me!" He said, "Oh, for real? I gave him that look, and he said he was sorry to hear that. He told me that he hated to see me hurting, and I pondered to myself why Arthur was there because he never really cared about me. I asked him again," Why are you here"? I said, "It seems mighty funny that you showed up at the right time of a breakup"! I asked him if he and Phil had planned it. He said no way and that he and Phil had not talked.

By now, we were at the corner of my street, where the playground was; I was sitting on the swing, and he was standing beside me. I was silent again, thinking about how Phil had just broken up with me and how I would have to start over or be by myself. I got upset all over again and began to cry. Arthur said, "Are you really that upset over him? "Why are you crying over him?" I remember I looked into Arthur's face and said, "Because he's a great guy!" I told him that Phil had been there for me since I found out I was pregnant, stuck by my side the whole time. Anything I asked for, he would provide or at least attempt to provide. He helped prepare for the baby to come, and after my baby was born, he was there to see about anything I needed. I further told him that if I had to take my baby to the emergency, he was there; if she needed medicine, he was there; when my VCR broke, he went and brought me a brand new one, and he bought me an expensive purse that was over $300, and when he thought I lost it he went and bought me two more. Arthur stepped back and said, "Well, I think I might want to date him!" We both laughed, which was his intention, to make me laugh. He then asked me if I cared about him and loved him, and I told him, "Yeah, I think I do!" Arthur said, "Well, it will be alright; it will all work out." He hugged me, wiped my tears, and said, "Let us get out of this cold." We walked back to my house, and he stayed a few more minutes playing with Sharayle and left.

CHAPTER 13 | THE ATTEMPTS

I was extremely devastated. I could not believe that, once again, I was in a position where I thought I was in a good relationship, thinking that if things went well, we could even start a family and then get married. But No! Boom, a breakup! It always seems as if men are never sure of themselves, so they always go out seeking to ensure they are making the right decision. At first, I thought I would be OK, and I just brushed it off, thinking that's his choice! I kept telling myself that I was going to be OK and that I had more important things to worry about, like taking care of my baby, trying to go back to school to finish my bachelor's degree, and trying to work on getting a career and other important things

However, I found myself constantly thinking about Phil.

I often wondered what he was doing, and I started checking myself for all the things that I perhaps could have done better or things I did wrong. Phil would say I had a bad attitude and was always snappy or smart-mouthed. Therefore, I had a reflecting moment. I would get angry and go back to reflecting again; it was a roller coaster, a yo-yo affair in my brain. At times, I would talk to a few people, some of my male cousins, trying to get their perspective and telling them how Phil wanted to show me a picture of the new girl. To my surprise, they said Phil was around telling them about it and showed them the girls' pictures. I could not believe it! I heard their opinion, so they told me she was cute. I asked, "So she looks better than me?" They tried not to hurt my feelings and said, "You're both cute." I started fussing, and my male cousin asked me if I wanted him to beat him up. At first, I pondered and was about to say, "Well, yes," but then I said, "No, no, that's not going to help anything."

I later spoke with my grandmother about it; she was sweet and the greatest listener. She gave short opinions. She told me that he should have understood that I needed a little time, that I just had the baby, and that he shouldn't have gotten so upset, and he knew that it was not right to go and get a girlfriend that soon. She further stated, "He should have understood, and he did not need to bring her to church around you because he wouldn't have liked that if he had been in your position." These were words of wisdom from a loving grandmother.

Lastly, I remember talking to my mom. I shared what happened and how I felt. She spoke these words of volume to me. She said, "Well, if you really like him and care about him the way it seems like you do, and if you believe he is worth fighting for, then try to win him back, but do not be a fool. If he doesn't want you, he doesn't want you, and there is nothing you can do about that, but if you give it a shot, then at least you'll know you gave it a try." I said, "Well, I do not know if it is worth trying. I am not begging anyone to be with me because I do not want to look weak and foolish."

My mother asked me if I loved him, and I thought about it for a minute and told her yes, but maybe we were not meant to be together." She said, "Well, tell you what, maybe you should write down on one side of the paper all the things you like about him that's good and then write down on the other side all the things you do not like that are bad about him, and if the good outweighs the bad, then there's your answer whether it is worth fighting for or not." That sounded profound, so I got up, got my notebook, and sat on her bed while she watched TV, and I began to think about all of Phil's good and bad. By the time I finished, I had a whole page and another column full of what I liked and was good about Phil, as well as a very short list of things that got on my nerves.

I was excited to share what I had with my mother, and she said, "Well, it looks like you have your answer." I told her, "Yes, I do, Mom; however, I am not about to be a fool. I will make a few attempts to get him back, and if he doesn't change, then it is not meant to be." Like they say, "If you love someone, let them go; if they come back to you, then it was meant to be."

Attempt #1: First, I called Phil on the phone to tell him that I wanted to talk to him and let him know that I truly apologize for my bad attitude or if he felt I was being mean or did not appreciate him. I wanted him to know that this was never my intention and that I truly appreciate everything he had done. I told him that he had been my rock all these months, how I loved that he loved my daughter, treated her as his own, provided for her, and was my answered prayer. He listened and said that was nice, and he appreciated me telling him and letting him know this. I told him I did not want to be with anyone else but Him. He made sketchy comments and said, "Oh, you are not seeing anyone else, you not dating anyone else, you have just been sitting at home?" At that moment, I felt offended. I hoped he did not think I was sitting here twiddling my thumbs and waiting on him. He must have forgotten I am not waiting on anybody. I had to let him know. I went out and had a couple of guys ask for my number. I told him that I had people I could call, but I was saying I would rather be with him. He said, "Well, I see you have not been to church." I said, "Because you were talking about bringing that girl to church, and I am trying to contain myself." I told him that I did not want to see her, and I thought it was very rude of him to want to bring her there. He said he thought about it and decided not to bring her to church, so I told him that was a good decision. Phil also said, "Well, if we do get back together, I am not coming as your boyfriend." I was not sure what that meant, so he had me puzzled by it.

Attempt #2: By now, I-had to be more creative. I wanted to give him something to remember my daughter, to remind him that he was the only dad that she knew. I went to the mall and saw that they could take photos and create T-shirts, buttons, and photo frames at a moment's notice, so I took a picture with my daughter. I had a T-shirt made that said "daddy's girls," as well as a button that he could put on his shirt, pants, or jacket, and a keychain that also said daddy's girl. I called him and told him I had something that I wanted to give him. I asked if I could come by his house and present it to him. Phil agreed, and I brought him the gift. I believe he was surprised and choked up on his words while staring at the T-shirt. I asked him if he would really wear the T-shirt, and excitedly, he said, "Of course, I'll wear this!" He also pinned the button to his pants. I asked him if he liked it and he said he loved it! Phil thanked me, and I did not press the issue to stay too long or say too much; I left and went on my way. Later that day, I called him to say hi and asked if his new girlfriend saw his button. He said yes, but she was not his girlfriend; they were dating. I said, "Oh, ok, well, what did she say?" He told me she just said my daughter was beautiful. We said a few more things and got off the phone.

Attempt #3: Phil and I would always joke about whether I could cook. Most of the time, either my father cooked, my mother cooked, or his mother cooked, or we went out to eat. I told him I could cook, but I was not claiming to be a great cook; however, I could make a few things. People always say, "A Way to a man's heart is through his stomach," so this was my next try.

I invited Phil over to have something to eat. No one was home, so I made a pot roast with vegetables and potatoes, some macaroni and cheese, and some Jiffy cornbread with some Kool-Aid. Phil stopped by and tore that food up, smacking lips & licking fingers. He was pleased, enjoyed the meal, and asked me why I had not done this before. I told him that it was because I never had time and that I just needed a little breathing room to catch up on myself, & my thoughts. I told him that I just needed to learn to organize my time.

My next step was inviting him to my mother's birthday party in about two weeks. He told me he was unsure if he could make it because he might have plans that weekend. I told him I would love for him to come and that I would be looking for him.

Attempt # 3 ½: About a week later, I called Phil to see if I could stop by to see him and talk if he was not busy. He agreed, and I made it over to his house. His mom was in the kitchen and was very happy to see me. We talked for a minute, and then Phil and I went down to the basement, where they had set up a little family area with a couch and TV. We sat down, and I started pouring out my heart again, but I was face to face this time. I wanted him to see the sincerity on my face; I wanted him to truly hear my heart. I apologized for seeming to be mean or seemingly uninterested. I told him I just wanted him to understand that I never wanted anyone else; I just needed to get used to being a mother and having a relationship because that was a lot. I told him I truly loved him and did not see myself being with anyone else but him. Phil said, "I see you trying, and I appreciate all you are doing." He said, "I told you if we get back together, I will not come as your boyfriend." I told him that I did not understand what that meant. Phil repeated, "If we get back together, I am not coming as a boyfriend." We were eye to eye, sitting close on the couch, and he looked like he was about to kiss me. Suddenly, his doorbell rang, and now his mother was calling him upstairs. This startled him, and he said, "OH… man, I forgot she was coming over here." I asked him who, and he told me that it was the girl he was dating. Of course, I was getting pissed off because I asked him if he was busy and if I could come by; he never said that someone was coming over. He explained that he was supposed to play bingo but thought it was later. I chuckled and asked him, "Do you guys play bingo like old people?" He answered yes and told me to wait in the basement and that he would be right back.

He went upstairs, and I sat in the basement for a few minutes. Then, I started pacing the floor, wondering what he was upstairs explaining to her. I wondered if he would tell her I was there, and then I thought she had to see my car; I knew he would not bring her down here. I thought he was probably trying to come up with a lie!

I waited a few minutes, then decided to go upstairs. Phil was about to get busted, and she would see me! All of this was going through my mind. I quietly walked up the stairs, and his mom was still in the kitchen. I said, "OK, I will see you later, Ms. Z," and she said, "OK." I walked towards the living room, and there Phil was, face to face with the girl, looking like he was trying to explain to her. I stopped right beside both of them. She was taller than me, about Phil's height, and I said, "Oh hello, you must be so and so; I heard all about you; nice to finally meet you." She did not respond, so I looked at Phil. I was close up on his side, and he looked at me, not knowing what to say, so I said, "Well, OK, I guess I will see you and talk to you later. Bye." I walked out the door and drove home, wondering how his night would go.

CHAPTER 14 | OTHER PEOPLE

I was talking to other people when Phil and I were taking a break, just not my baby's daddy; I had gone on a few dates a few times. I met a nice guy, and I told him my story. He was still interested and asked if he could come and see me. I allowed him to visit once to watch a movie with my daughter in her playpen. He was nice, but I was numb; I did not want to start over because I knew who I wanted. There was also an older guy who was friends with my older sister's boyfriend; he was Jamaican and a nice man, but I was not interested in older men. My sister and her boyfriend kept telling me how much he liked me from the first time he saw me. I went to dinner with him once, but again, I was numb and uninterested.

Then there was my old flame, my first boyfriend. He had just gotten out of his situation and started calling me again and hanging out. He wanted to be my daughter's godfather and still let me know that he would be there for me and that we could be together if I wanted him. I told him that I did not think we would work well with each other or clash as partners, but we're good at being friends, and I truly appreciated him. He was dating someone else anyway, but I invited him to my mom's birthday party.

Sometime later, my mom told me she had seen Arthur and told him about her party. She told him if he wanted to come by, he could. I said, "Mom, why did you invite him?" She said, "I do not know. I just let him know I was having a party. Plus, I thought you and Phil had broken up." I said, "We did, but I also invited him to the party." My mom said, "Well, he's probably not coming anyway." She was talking about Arthur.

The night before the party, I asked Phil if he could attend the birthday party; he told me he was still unsure. I told him, "Well, just to let you know, my ex will be there with his girlfriend, and my mom may have mentioned to Arthur about her party, but he probably will not show up; however, I just wanted you to know and not be surprised if you come."

The night of the party, I wanted to look cute. I got my hair, nails, and toes done, picked out a cute outfit, smelled good, and went to the party. A lot of my friends, cousins, and family were there. My ex did show up with his girlfriend; he asked me to dance a couple of rounds, and I kept staring at the door, but there was no Phil. By the end of the party, when everyone was about to leave, I saw the doors opening, and I got excited and thought it was Phil! To my disappointment, Arthur showed up at the last minute. My ex had already left, which was a good thing because the two of them might have clashed. Arthur, of course, had already been drinking and stayed to help us clean up. He wanted a ride back to my side of town, and of course, my mother agreed to give him a ride.

Once we got to our house, he asked us if he could come in to see my daughter, and of course, I said yes. My mom went upstairs to go to bed. We went down into the basement. I had one of my little cousins babysitting, and they also went upstairs to sleep. Arthur came in and looked at my daughter while she was asleep. He said a few words and then tried to push up on me. I said, "You can forget about it!" He left, but I heard knocking on my side window ten minutes later. It was Arthur asking if he could come back in. He said he could not get into his aunt's house, which was around the corner, and asked if he could stay for the night. I told him he would have to sleep on the couch and get up early to leave because he knows I cannot have anyone stay overnight. He agreed, but later, he came and got in my bed; I jumped up and went to the couch. Arthur said, "Now you know that's uncomfortable out there. You can sleep in here; we can be adults; I won't bother you; I'll sleep outside the cover." He was right; it was uncomfortable, so I returned to bed. He slept outside of the cover, and nothing happened. He left early in the morning. I was so disappointed that Phil did not show up or call me. It seems like the devil was trying to block my blessings and put Arthur in my way.

During this breakup, I sought advice from different people I trusted. I got a call from my Bestie, my cousin Marie, who joined the military and was stationed in Turkey then. I told her about the situation and how it tore me up inside. I told her I could not believe I was going through this again by another man. By this time, she had already gotten an annulment from her marriage from the guy who came home with her to visit back that summer when Phil and I went to the amusement park with them. It was a short marriage that did not work out. My cousin offered for my baby and me to come over to an all-expense paid trip to Turkey to hang out for a little while until I got my thoughts together. I thought she was joking at first. Turkey! I never imagined it. But she was serious! She said she would get our plane tickets! I thought about it, and I told her I did not want to mooch off of her, so I said, let me see how much money I could come up with. I was not working then; I was waiting for government assistance, but they had not paid me yet, and I knew I was supposed to be getting back pay for a few months. I could have a decent lump sum of money and take this trip.

I spoke with Phil later that week, and I told him about the proposal offered to me and that I may take this opportunity to get away from my hometown and get a new perspective on my life and circumstances. I told him that I wanted to get a chance to do things I never thought I could do: A chance to see the world. He listened and said, "Wow, all the way to Turkey, huh?" He asked,

"How long would you be gone?" I said, "I do not know." He said, "How soon are you trying to leave?" I said, "As soon as I can get my money together."

The offer gave me a bit of excitement, took me out of my dump, and also gave me a plan if it did not work with Phil or if he was just into that girl and did not want to be with me. However, deep down, I still wanted my man back.

CHAPTER 15 | THE FINAL ATTEMPT

It was the last attempt to win Phil back.

My older sister was going out of town for one night. It was on a Friday night, and I devised a plan. I thought I would stay the night at her house, get my mom to babysit, and then persuade Phil to come by and see me. I told him the night before that I would have the place to myself and that I had a babysitter. I told him I missed him and that he owed me for not attending my mother's birthday party. I also told him he would not regret it if he came because I had something really special waiting for him.

Phil told me he was supposed to go to a bowling party with the girl, so I told him to come by after he dropped her off because he wouldn't want to miss this opportunity. I would hate for my

145

sister's boyfriend's friend to show up at the house (I was referring to the older guy who liked me), so I had to let him know there was still an opportunity for someone else on my end, too. Phil told me it would be around 11 pm or a little later after the bowling party if he could come by. I told him not to make me a promise and not show up because I would not ask again. He said, "ok, I will try and make it."

When I got to my sister's house, I began setting the atmosphere by showering, lighting candles, putting on sweet-smelling fragrances, and a nice lingerie with a sexy overall. I started watching the clock 9:30, 10:30, 11:00! I was biting my nails and praying, saying, "This is it; I am no one's fool. If he does not want me, I will let it go because I tried. If he does not come tonight, that is my sign that it is over and not meant to be."

It was 11:15 pm, and the tears began to roll down my face as that lump settled in my throat, and my heart ached. I heard a faint knock at the door as I was about to give up. I sat very still and was holding my breath to make sure I listened to what I thought I heard. Knock, knock! There it was again! This time, I jumped up, wiped my face, looked at myself in the mirror to ensure I was

OK, and then said, "Who is it?" As if I did not know. He said, "It's Phil." I did my quiet, happy dance, praise danced, and opened the door. Phil walked in, we hugged, and he asked if I was alright. I said, "Yeah, I thought you were not coming and had stood me up." I told him I was about to sleep, but I was lying. I knew I would have been crying all night. He reminded me that he told me he would be late after the bowling party.

We sat on the couch, and I asked him about his night. He cut me off and said, "You said you had something for me," as he looked at me like I was his last meal. I responded, "Well, that something is me!" Phil pushed up on me and kissed me, and once again, he said, "I told you when I came back, I was not coming back as your boyfriend." I stared at him, looking puzzled, not understanding what he meant. Then, he kissed me again passionately on my lips, neck, and chest and guided me to the bedroom.

Phil stayed with me through the night. I told him that my uncles were throwing a cabaret party on Saturday and that I would love for him to accompany me. He said, "Okay, yes, I would like to go." I was shocked when he said he had no plans. Of course, I was all grins that Saturday morning when he left.

When my sister came home later that day, she asked me what was going on with me. I told her I was happy. I got ready for the party that night, and Phil said he would pick me up. I said, "We are going on a date!" Again, I smiled.

The Cabaret Party

Phil came and picked me up, and I was smiling from ear to ear. I ensured I looked good, smelled good, and did not care about that other girl. We got to the party, and the music was playing. Many of my family were already there, and we danced, laughed, talked, and did some drinking because it was a party! Everyone was happy to see Phil and me together.

When it was getting close to the end of the night, the party was just about winding down. Phil had been drinking and slurring over his words by now. We were slow dancing, and he kept saying, "I told you when I came back to you that I would not be coming back as your boyfriend." I said, "Phil, you keep saying that; what does that mean?" He ignored my question at first, and then once we stopped dancing and sat down at the table with no one else around us, Phil turned to me and said, "Stacey, will you marry me?" I said, "Wait, what did you just say?" And he said it again. I responded, "Yeah, right, you are just playing." Phil looked me in my eyes and told me he was not playing and was dead serious! He said, "The Lord told me you are supposed to be my wife!" My eyes were filled with water, and I said, "YES!" We hugged and kissed, but suddenly, Phil said, "Do not tell anyone yet!" I said, "Are you kidding me? Wow, why would you tell me not to tell anybody?" I told him I knew he was playing, and that was not cool or funny. Phil tried to calm me down so that he could explain. He said he wanted to wait, and we will tell everyone later. I told him he would have to ask me again the next day because he had been drinking, and I wanted him to be good and sober when he asked me. I told Phil I also wanted him to ask my parents, and I wanted him on one knee. Phil agreed and said he would do it all, that he loved me, and that he would ask me repeatedly.

I did not say anything to anyone at the party. I was in shock and did not think it was real. Phil told me not to say anything, so I thought, well, I do not want to look like a fool, so I will be quiet. However, in the next few minutes, one of my cousins congratulated me and said, "So you guys are getting married?" I stared in shock and asked, "Why would you say that?" They said that Phil told them that and that he was telling everyone. I thought about how he just sat here and told me not to say anything. He said he wanted us to say it together but was running around telling everybody he asked me to marry him! I just laughed it off and told them that he had been drinking and that we would see what he said tomorrow.

151

Stay tuned for the release of VOL #2 to find out if Phil was serious about his proposal and whether "This love was the real love

About The Author

Mrs. T. Jackson is a remarkable woman dedicated to serving her family and community and doing the things of God. She is a devoted mother of two adult children whom she has raised with great care and attention, instilling in

them the importance of a strong connection with the Lord. She is also a caring wife to her retired Air Force Master Sergeant husband, and they have been together for over 31 years, sharing a beautiful bond of love and companionship.

Mrs. Jackson's unwavering faith in God inspires everyone who knows her. She has a kind heart and always sees the best in people, so she is loved and respected by all who cross her path. Mrs. Jackson became an ordained minister because of her deep devotion to God and understanding of the importance of intercessory prayer. She prays diligently for those who cannot pray for themselves. Her prayers have brought miracles to many lives.

Throughout her life, Mrs. Jackson has served her community in various roles, including children's minister, youth leader, preschool teacher, religious education coordinator, dance ministry, and usher. She has also led a small community Bible study group in her home and shared the Word of God in several churches.

Mrs. Jackson has earned several degrees, including an Associate degree in Business Administration, a Bachelor of Science degree in Human Development, a Master of Science degree in Theology, and a master's certificate in Family and Marriage Therapy and Human Resource Development. She is always eager to learn more by reading and researching various subjects, making her wise and knowledgeable.

Mrs. Jackson has a heart to serve and share God's love and grace with everyone. She wants all people to know God's will and purpose for their lives and be saved.

Mrs. Jackson currently works at the Veteran Health Administration in the Human Resource Department, where she helps bring happiness to people as they join the team to serve veterans.

Her work is a testament to her commitment to serving others, and she is a shining example of what it means to live a life of purpose and meaning.

This Love "Love That Covers A Multitude of Sins."

This Love "Love That Covers A Multitude of Sins."